Inclusive Education in Low-Income Countries

A resource book for
teacher educators, parent trainers
and community development workers

Lilian Mariga, Roy McConkey and Hellen Myezwa

Acknowledgements

Save the Children (UK) supported the development of the Inclusive Education Project in Lesotho and the Norwegian Association for Persons with Developmental Disabilities (NFU) along with Operation Days Work (ODW), Norway, the work in Zanzibar and Tanzania. The support of the respective Ministries of Education in these countries is gratefully acknowledged, along with that of the Parent and Friends Associations: LSMHP and ZAPPD. Our colleagues Lineo Phachaka (Lesotho) and Mpaji Ali Maalim (Zanzibar) deserve particular mention for their wise counsel and hard work in implementing Inclusive Education. We are very grateful to Atlas Alliance and to University of Witwatersrand, School of Therapeutic Sciences for sponsoring the printing of the book.

Throughout the book we draw upon the UNESCO publication: *Understanding and Responding to Children's Needs in Inclusive Classrooms: A Guide for Teachers*.

Published by Atlas Alliance, Schweigaardsgate 12, P.O. Box 9217 Grønland, 0134 Oslo, Norway; and Disability Innovations Africa, Disability Studies Programme, School of Health and Rehabilitation Sciences, University of Cape Town

© Lilian Mariga, Roy McConkey and Hellen Myezwa, 2014

ISBN 978-0-9870203-4-5

First published 2014

Citation: Mariga, L., McConkey, R. and Myezwa, H. (2014) *Inclusive Education in Low-Income Countries: A resource book for teacher educators, parent trainers and community development workers*. Cape Town: Atlas Alliance and Disability Innovations Africa.

Production by Bronwen Dachs Müller, Cape Town

Printed by Megadigital, Cape Town

Further enquiries about the book: Disability Innovations Africa, Disability Studies Programme, School of Health and Rehabilitation Sciences, University of Cape Town, Private Bag X3, Rondebosch 7701

Download the electronic version of the book here:
http://www.eenet.org.uk/ or http://www.atlas-alliansen.no/English

All rights reserved. No part of this publication may be reproduced or transmitted, in any form or by any means, without prior permission from the publishers.

Foreword

Many beautiful words have been written about inclusive education but it is rare to come across a book which is not only based on a wealth of grassroots experience but comes at a particularly opportune moment.

In the 20 years that have passed since Salamanca, it is countries of the South that have shown the way to inclusive education. I had the good fortune of visiting Lesotho schools when Lillian Mariga was helping to launch its pilot programme in the mid-1990s. What I saw there convinced me that inclusive education could succeed, given political will, good leadership, preparation of teachers and parental and community support. Since then, there have been authentic reports of successful projects from many countries, including Bangladesh, India, Kenya, Laos, South Africa, Tanzania, Uganda, Vietnam and Zambia, amongst others[1].

That's the good news, greatly enriched by this book. The bad news is that children with disabilities have not benefited from Education for All or the Millennium Development Goal of free primary education by 2015. One third of the 61 million children still excluded from school are children with disabilities.

This shameful discrimination cannot be allowed to continue. The 126 countries that have so far ratified the UN Convention on the Rights of Persons with Disabilities[2] are now accountable in international law both to the UN and to their own citizens to publish national plans to implement its principles and articles. Furthermore, there is already a strong commitment within the UN and the international community to ensure that minorities who have not benefited from the Millennium Development Goals will be fully included in the revised goals now being discussed. The emphasis in future is likely to be on the reduction of poverty-related inequalities, the quality of education at all levels and on teacher training.

Everything now depends on civil society such as parent groups and Disabled Persons Organisations putting pressure on their governments to implement the Convention in full. Advocates for inclusive education need to ensure that priority is given not only to enabling children with disabilities to attend but to benefit from school by applying what has been learned from books such as this to supporting teachers, families and the children themselves.

If information is power, the internet bestows it in abundance. Governments are currently submitting detailed reports on their actions to implement the Convention to the Disabled Persons Committee of the UN High Commission on Human Rights, all but one of whose members is a disabled person. DPOs can make their own submissions to the Committee and its final report, which will be available on the internet, will provide a powerful tool for advocacy[3].

The journey towards inclusive education may never end but this book will provide a trustworthy road map along the way.

Peter Mittler, CBE
Emeritus Professor of Special Educational Needs, University of Manchester, England

1 Rieser, R. (2012) Implementing Inclusive Education: A Commonwealth Guide to Implementing Article 24 of the UN Convention on the Rights of Persons with Disabilities (2nd edn.) London: Commonwealth Secretariat.
2 Listed on http://www.un.org/disabilities
3 http://www.ohchr.org/EN/HRBodies/CRPD/Pages/CRPDIndex.aspx

Contents

Part 1: Introducing Inclusive Education

Introduction	1
Experiences from Africa	2
The authors	4
The book as a resource for educators	5
DVD – Inclusion in Action	11
Chapter 1: Planning for Inclusive Education	12
The Foundations of Inclusive Education	13
Creating Social Capital	17
Administrative Structures to Support Inclusion	19
Chapter 2: Introducing Inclusive Education	24
Defining Inclusive Education	27
International support for Inclusive Education	30
Prerequisites for Inclusive Education	35
The benefits of Inclusive Education	37

Part 2: Promoting Inclusion

Chapter 3: Family Involvement	40
Overcoming the myths of disability	43
Home-based interventions	45
Parent support groups	47
Home-school partnerships	48
Chapter 4: Promoting Advocacy and Empowerment	52
Parent advocacy	55
Disabled People's Organisations	57
Advocacy and disabled youth	59
Chapter 5: Involving Local Communities	62
Rationale for community involvement	63
Changing community perceptions of disability	64
Examples of community education	66
Chapter 6: Engaging with Community Health Services	71
Partnerships with primary health care workers	73
Partnerships with Health service personnel and disability specialists	75
Partnerships with Community-Based Rehabilitation (CBR)	77

Part 3: Creating Inclusive Schools

Chapter 7: Conducting a feasibility study for Inclusive Education	80
Preparing for a feasibility study	81
Conducting a feasibility study	82
Examples of findings	87
Chapter 8: Preparing Teachers	90
Providing in-service teacher education	92
Training manuals for teachers	96
Schools learning from one another	99
Chapter 9: Supporting Pupils to Learn	101
Communication	103
Assessing children's difficulties	104
Individual Education Plans	107
Assisting students to learn	108
Individual help	112
Chapter 10: Managing Inclusive Classrooms	114
Including everyone	116
The layout of the classroom	117
Lesson planning	118
Child-to-child/peer tutoring	119
Managing disruptive behaviours	120
Chapter 11: Future Challenges	124
Adapting the curriculum	125
Evaluating Inclusive Education	129
References and Further Reading	133

Introduction

The history of people with disabilities has been dominated by their isolation and exclusion. The long fight towards inclusion – and inclusive education in particular – started not many years ago. Most were powerless to control their own destiny. Their participation in society has been the object of other's actions. In many countries their disability policies have a substantial element of protection and charity but not the right to equalisation of opportunities.

This book highlights the process of change that is underway internationally. The equalisation of opportunities requires new processes through which the various systems of society such as health services and education are delivered. It means the right for people with disabilities to remain in their communities and to receive the schooling and social supports they need within the ordinary structures available in local communities. Strong advocacy is needed for this to happen. In particular parents need to be empowered, communities mobilised and professionals trained in new ways of working: hence this book.

Drawing on experiences in Africa, the book describes the issues to be considered when it comes to implementing inclusive strategies: the processes to be followed and the roles of different sectors, such as people with disabilities, parents, policy makers, educationalists, health and community development professionals and crucially, society at large. As such four chapters focus on the generic foundations that benefit the inclusion of persons with disabilities in general as well as particularly in schools. This includes family involvement, enhanced community services, the promotion of advocacy and community education strategies.

The remaining chapters then focus on inclusive education approaches within schools. The book covers the diverse elements in implementing an inclusive education strategy from the introduction of the process through to evaluation, consolidation and extension within the education system. The different chapters provide detail on discrete parts of the process. We describe how feasibility studies can be undertaken as a way of creating awareness among schools; uncovering the attitudes of teachers and parents, discovering whether resources – human, material and financial – are available, and whether the school environments are user-friendly. Devising an inclusive policy and preparing an implementation plan provides a guide for actions, such as the training of teachers. This is covered through in-service courses as well as the inclusion of different support strategies within schools. Other chapters describe how teachers can assess students' strengths and barriers to learning as a basis for developing Individual Education Plans (IEP) for learners with different abilities. It further explains teaching strategies that have proved effective in the management of inclusive classrooms.

Global Initiatives

Inclusive education seeks to put an end to discriminatory practices that both consciously and unconsciously exclude some children from receiving an appropriate education and is therefore an important strategy for the attainment of the broader "Education for All" (EFA) agenda set by world leaders in 2001. Likewise one of the eight Millennium Development Goals agreed by 189 nations under the United Nations Development Programme (2000) was to "achieve universal primary education by 2015". This target is unlikely to be met as some 61 million children world-wide and over 30 million in sub-Saharan Africa remain out-of-school. UNESCO estimates that around one-third have disabilities. Further details at: http://www.un.org/millenniumgoals/education.shtml

The new millennium also heralded new thinking as to what it means to have a disability. The World Health Organisation in its International Classification of Functioning (2002) defines it as "an outcome of the interaction between a person with impairment and the environmental and attitudinal barriers that he/she faces (p.16)'. Hence improvements in the lifestyle of persons with a disability have to go beyond remediating their impairments which has been the dominant focus of special education and therapeutic services.

Introducing inclusive practices into segregated education systems means influencing all levels of the education system as well as associated service providers such as health and social services. International experience has shown that introducing inclusive practices cannot be done without introducing major system changes. The long term objective of creating a society with inclusive education, relates to the opening up of all regular schools and programmes so they welcome, accommodate and meet the learning needs of all members of the local community.

Experiences from Africa

Given this global context, we write to share the information derived from three African countries - Lesotho, Tanzania, and Zanzibar - which have introduced Inclusive Education and the significant achievements that have been realised at a relatively low cost. Their programmes have been internationally evaluated. All three projects were initiated and implemented under the leadership and guidance of Lilian Mariga in the period (1990 – 2010).

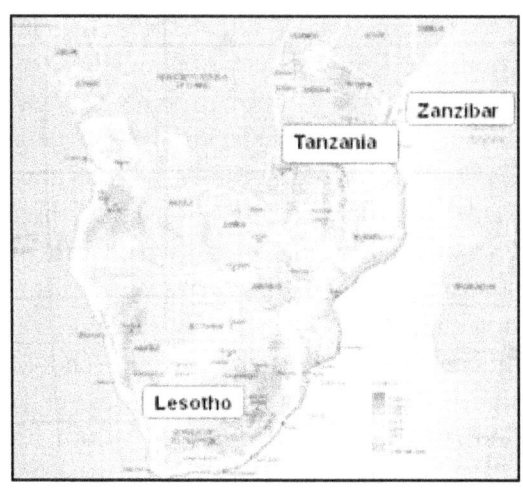

Lesotho

Lesotho is a small mountainous country, surrounded by South Africa. Harsh winters and high altitudes make much of the country inaccessible in winter. The population is estimated at 2 million, mostly consisting of Basotho peoples whose language is Sesotho. For over a hundred years, until independence in 1966, Lesotho was a British Protectorate. Throughout its history, Lesotho's economy and stability has been inextricably linked to that of South Africa where a quarter of the workforce has sought employment.

The provision of education in Lesotho is a joint venture between the Government, churches and the community (see http://www.sacmeq.org/education-lesotho.htm). In 2010, there were around 345,000 children enrolled in primary and secondary schools, which is about a 75% enrolment of the child population aged 5-14 years. The main reasons for non-enrolment are poor public transport and long distances from schools coupled with families being unable to afford school fees. The number of children dropping out of school increases markedly up to Grade 7. The pupil-teacher ratio is estimated at 40:1 in primary school and about 75% of teachers are qualified.

Nonetheless the inclusive education programme that was developed there in the 1990s onwards has shown that even without a wealth of resources, major changes can be brought about in the educational system to increase access for children with disabilities and other vulnerable groups. Lesotho is a fine example of inclusion resulting from an interaction between government schools, NGOs and local communities' a partnership well suited to nurturing inclusive education (Khatleli et al., 1995).

Zanzibar

Zanzibar is an archipelago off the coast of Tanzania consisting of two main islands – Unguja and Pemba. With a predominantly Muslim population of just under a million, an estimated 60% live in poverty with an average life expectancy of 56 years. Although primary education is free and the gross net enrolment is close to 100%, attendance rates are around 70% with over 130,000 children of school-going age outside the educational system (see http://www.saccmeg.org/education-zanzibar.htm).

The government is committed to education for all but faces many infrastructural challenges in achieving this target by 2015, including an acute shortage of classrooms, inadequate and poorly trained teachers, large class sizes and high teacher: pupil ratios (officially 1:40 but extending to 1:80 in underserved areas), and inadequate teaching and learning materials as most expenditure goes to teacher salaries. International donors contribute around 70% of the education budget.

Formally the education of children with special educational needs began in 1998 with the formation of a special education unit within the Ministry of Education and Vocational Training, and the establishment by 2004 of five units attached to mainstream schools. However, the most recent policy document emphasised inclusion within mainstream schools and with financial support from NFU, Norway and the leadership of Lilian Mariga and her local counter-part Mpaji Ali Maalim, inclusive education is being implemented.

Tanzania

The United Republic of Tanzania has a population of nearly 40 million, with agriculture the mainstay of the economy. Income disparity is large and there are many families, especially in rural areas that depend on subsistence farming. There is universal access to primary education and over 8 million children are enrolled in around 12,000 primary schools with a pupil-teacher ratio estimated at 1:55. However the drop-out rate exceeds 20% and is greater with boys than girls (see http://www.sacmeq.org/education-tanzania.htm).

The Ministry of Education has a Department of Special Education and small numbers of children and youth with disabilities and other special needs were placed in special schools and institutions but many had no access to education. With financial assistance from NFU and ODW in Norway and working through the Tanzanian Association for Mental Handicap, a pilot project on Inclusive Education ran from 2001 to 2004. This involved the sensitisation of communities, parents and local schools while working in close collaboration the government and officials in the Ministry of Education. A feasibility study was undertaken in selected schools along with the production of training materials for teachers in Kiswahili along with the provision of training courses. Also intensive lobbying locally and nationally helped put children's rights on the platform and ensured that disabled and other vulnerable children have equal opportunities in education.

The Authors

The three authors have direct experience of working in many low-income countries but especially within Africa.

Lilian Mariga's strength is in 'hands-on' work. She first trained as a nurse and a midwife, then as an educator in disability issues in the USA. On returning to her native Zimbabwe, she designed a Home Based learning programme, worked in CBR and in Inclusive education which involved communities, leaders, different service providers and policy makers. She became a consultant with Save the Children (UK) and later for NFU (Norwegian Association for Persons with Developmental Disabilities) during which time she introduced inclusive education in Lesotho, Tanzania and Zanzibar as well as working also to strengthen parent associations. The book is based largely on the practises, experiences, and lessons she has gained over the past 30 years.

Professor Roy McConkey first worked with Lilian in the 1980s on the development of video-based training materials in Zimbabwe sponsored by Irish Foreign Aid. Subsequently he was involved with UNESCO and the Guyana Community-Based Rehabilitation Programme in various inclusive education initiatives and with Lilian Mariga in the documenting the projects in Lesotho and Zanizabar. He has undertaken consultancies for WHO, UNICEF and various international NGOs in some 20 countries around the world. He is Emeritus Professor of Developmental Disabilities at the University of Ulster, Northern Ireland.

Professor Hellen Myezwa is Head of Physiotherapy in the Faculty of Health Sciences at the University of Witwatersrand, Johannesburg. She has extensive experience of pioneering community-based rehabilitation in her home country of Zimbabwe and in developing home based care programmes where the concept of community participation and empowerment was strongly promoted. She has a long involvement in the training of personnel in health services and of working in partnership with teachers and schools. Her current research focuses on the impact of HIV and AIDs in the disability sector.

The Book as a Resource for Educators

When initiating inclusive education in these three African countries, many people and professionals across different sectors raised the same questions, such as:

- Is inclusive education possible in developing countries where there are few resources?
- Is inclusive education really about including all groups?
- What is the difference between Inclusive education, integration and special education?
- Is inclusion appropriate for severely disabled children, including those who are deaf and blind? Is inclusive education very costly?
- How can developing countries with limited resources manage to start inclusive education?

This book is our attempt to provide answers to these and other questions. But we want to emphasise that all the above questions can only be addressed when one uses a holistic but realistic strategy. This means using a participatory approach throughout, encouraging multi-disciplinary working among professionals, creating awareness within the whole community, soliciting the cooperation and collaboration of associated services and gaining the involvement of policy makers. In essence the aim is to transform the way local societies treat people with disabilities: accepting their differences while providing them with the opportunities for a fulfilled life.

> Ministries of Education in member states and with organisations in Civil Society will facilitate among all role players the development of a common understanding of inclusive education where all children learn together in their neighbourhood.

Draft Southern Africa Regional Inclusive Education Strategy, Secretariat for the African Decade of Disabled Persons, 2012

The secret of a successful inclusive education programme is in the training of teachers, the preparation of conducive learning environments in schools, the empowerment of parents, and the education of community members and professionals in allied service systems. It is important also, to keep the policy makers well informed through running workshops for them and giving them progress reports on regular basis. The more they understand, the more supportive they become. When policy makers understand issues of different disabilities, their causes, their rights and inclusiveness, issues of inclusive policy are then better handled.

The book is by no means a comprehensive text book on inclusive education. Rather it is intended primarily as a resource for people who have a training and education role in their community; foremost of which are teacher educators. But we take this to include practicing teachers and head teachers in local schools as well as those based in teacher-training colleges or with responsibility for the in-service training of teachers. We hope the book will prove useful also to trainers of health and social service personnel and those working in community development as they too have a vital role to play in promoting greater inclusion of children with disabilities but they may feel less knowledgeable about inclusive education. Lastly the book should prove helpful to the leaders of disabled persons' organisations and of parent associations. They too have a key advocacy role with policy makers but also in ensuring their membership has a full understanding of the issues relating to inclusive education.

Our hope is to assist with raising up a cadre of leaders who can make change happen in their local communities. For all that inclusion needs to be underpinned by national policies, the reality can only be experienced locally. However leadership for inclusion require certain skills and qualities: in particular, good planning skills, attentive listening, being cooperative, having respect for others' opinions, participatory planning with other ministries and stake-holders but above all, consulting with the target groups and respect for their human rights.

The book provides readers with a basic overview of the main issues relating to the introduction and implementation of inclusive education at a local level. The content is presented in the form of suggested training strategies for communicating the main themes to the intended trainees and how they might be adapted for particular groups such as teachers, parents and community personnel. We also identify useful print or audio-visual materials that can be used in training sessions and which are available free-of-charge often via the Internet.

That said, the book is not prescriptive as any training must be tailored to the specific needs and circumstances of the local community. This can appear to be a daunting task but throughout our many years of working even in the most impoverished settings, we have been humbled by the quality of leadership shown by local personnel and their enthusiasm to make life better for people with disabilities and their families. By sharing their expertise and experiences through the pages of this book, we hope that many others will be enabled to join in creating more inclusive communities around the world.

Preparing Training Inputs

In this section we present some ideas for how the materials might be used as a resource for the preparation of training inputs to various stake-holders. We begin with some tips on preparing to organise and present any training inputs.

Training Needs

Having identified the group you will train, you must think about what they need to learn. Your previous experience of working with them will give you plenty of ideas, especially as you discuss the issues with your colleagues. The people who can contribute most to this discussion are those who have direct and recent experience of working in local communities. Another approach is to consult with several of the potential participants; asking them what they want to learn. For example, local people may want to know more about the impact on non-disabled children; parents could be more concerned about negative experiences their child might encounter in school, such as teasing and bullying. Equally though you need to beware of trying to cover too many different topics within the one training session or course. Try to identify priority needs and focus on these during the course.

Team work

Although one person could organise a training course, the workload is best shared by a team of two or three people. This has other advantages too – a wider range of talents are involved in the planning; the course can still continue if one person is ill or moves away and people can help each other if they encounter problems. It is worth exploring which colleagues might assist with the planning and delivery of the course. A mix of people from different backgrounds is ideal. We have organised courses with teachers, parents and disability activists as co-tutors.

Learning activities

People learn more if they are actively involved. Training is more than someone standing in front of a group talking. Here are some suggestions for various learning activities you can incorporate into your training sessions.

Sharing experiences: the group might be asked to recall their favourite play activities as children, as an introduction to a session on how children can learn through play. Or they could recall the different names which people with disabilities have been called as a beginning to a community education session.

Video: In many developing countries oral and visual communication is commonly used in preference to the written word. Visual learning is more effective because it helps people to understand the new knowledge they are being given and it can be practically explained. There are good video resources available that demonstrate inclusion in action. We have referred to these throughout the text and most are freely available or can be accessed via the Internet.

Brainstorming: Participants can be divided into small groups and asked to think of as many different ways learners can be helped with simple addition or to write their name. Likewise, they can list the different jobs around the school that a person with disabilities could do to demonstrate their abilities. These brainstorms are good for prompting people to come up with new ideas; some of which may not work but others will!

First-hand experiences: Participants could experience some of the effects of a disability and from this, gain a better understanding of what can be done to help. For example, tackling a task blindfolded or trying to learn a few words in a foreign language can bring home to people how difficult it can be for children to learn. Trying to move around the school in a wheelchair would help them realise problems in accessibility.

Making simple teaching aids: During the training session, time can be set aside to make simple aids that can help pupils learn in the classroom, such as thickening a pencil with cloth to help a child to write. Course organisers need to ensure that enough tools and materials are to hand for this. Participants should be encouraged to design them with a learner in mind and to try-out them out at school.

Discussions: Participants can be given a specific issue to discuss with one another and draw up their own conclusions. This is best done in groups of four to six people and their ideas can be reported back to the larger group: for example, the advantages and disadvantages of children with disabilities attending ordinary schools.

Role plays: Participants can act out a role play based on simulated or real experiences, such parents experiencing a 'bad' interview with a doctor or head teacher. Then they may re-enact it to show how it might have been done better. In both instances draw attention to the emotions experiences by the main characters.

Task setting: the group, or subgroups, can be set a particular task to do; for instance; devising a teaching plan for crossing a road safely or the steps involved in teaching children to recognise coins and bank notes. Better still, if participants have the chance to try out their plans with children or young people and report back to the group at a subsequent meeting.

Variety of experiences

People on training courses appreciate variety, especially if the course lasts a full day. Some ways of varying the learning experience include:

Guest speakers: local specialists could be invited to give a short talk to the group. Give the speaker detailed instructions on what you want them to cover; the time available and how their contribution fits in with the rest of the course. Ensure there is time left for them to answer the group's questions as this is often the most valuable part of these sessions.

Demonstrations: the group can see at first hand how to make a piece of equipment; or to test a child's hearing and so on. These live demonstrations may repeat what they have seen in the video but they will serve to make sure the message gets across.

Visual aids: Posters and flipcharts can be used to remind participants of key messages. Likewise, blackboards or large sheets of paper can be used to write up ideas that emerge from talks or group work. Indeed participants can make their own posters as part of one the learning activities.

Homework: the goal of training is to get people putting new ideas into practice. You need to plan for this to happen during the course. For example, participants can be expected to carry out 'new' activities with children and to report back at the next session on their experiences. Ideally the course tutors should try and visit the participants at school to observe how they are tackling the activity and to gain a better insight in the local circumstances. This will help you demonstrate how the lessons of the course can be applied in their setting.

Hand-outs: Simple take home leaflets will also help participants to remember points made during the course. These should recap the main learning points from the training and perhaps include details as to where further information is available. Photocopies are probably the quickest and cheapest way of producing simple leaflets.

Reviewing the course: During the course, the tutors should meet to review the past session and to plan the next. In this way, modifications can be made to the programme in the light of experiences. It is also a good idea to invite participants to give their reaction by getting them to answer two simple questions: 1) what have they got out of the course thus far?; and 2) what do they hope to get out of the remaining sessions?

Qualities of tutors

Our experience suggests that certain qualities are needed by people who are training others. They can be found among a wide range of people in addition to those who are usually considered to be 'trainers'. If people do not have these qualities they should strive to nurture them.

- Effective trainers are very familiar with the local culture. If they are expatriate workers they have been in the country for five or more years.

- They may be trained and experienced professionals but they are able and willing to step outside their particular specialism to provide 'multi-disciplinary' training opportunities.

Often they have been able to call on a network of contacts to supplement their knowledge and expertise of other disciplines.

- They are able communicators who form a ready rapport with the trainees.

- They are highly motivated to help people with disabilities and their families and provide inspiration to others.

- Last, but by no means least, they have a clear vision of the goals they wish to achieve and they have a plan for bringing them about.

Training Outcomes

Finally, how do we judge the success of training? Traditionally training in disability and education has been focused on equipping people with knowledge and skills. However a community-based approach must take a broader view and ensure that the training offered to communities and families produces at least three other important outcomes:

- It engenders positive attitudes and increases motivation to assist people with a disability.

- It changes the behaviour of family members and the community towards people with a disability.

- It encourages the development of local services through the initiatives of local people and further promotes their capacity to be self-reliant.

Of course all these outcomes apply equally to persons with a disability, which is why our training initiatives must actively embrace people with a disability as well.

How the book can be used by trainers

In the remainder of the book, each chapter is devoted to a main theme within the provision of inclusive education. The relevant background information is provided and suggestions are given as to how these messages might be communicated to participants attending the training. Readers will need to adapt this content according to the background of the people attending and the length of time set aside for the training, be it a one-hour session, half-a-day or a full-day. Equally certain themes are more relevant for some groups than others.

The entire book provides the content for a complete course aimed at introducing inclusive education especially to trainee teachers or to serving teachers as part of their in-service training. In these instances, the chapters provide the structure and content of suggested curriculum for a module that may last for 10 three-hour sessions. Of course, tutors will need to weave in local circumstances, policies and practices into their teaching but the major themes are summarised here.

The final pages of the book contain references to further reading and useful websites.

DVD: *Inclusion in Action*

A series of video programmes was produced to illustrate the introduction of the Inclusive Education in Zanzibar. This is available as a DVD free of charge from Atlas-Alliance at this website:

http://www.atlas-alliansen.no/English/How-can-we-contribute-to-Education-for-All

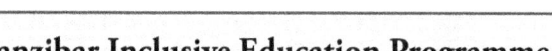

Also the programmes can be downloaded from YouTube. The content of each programme is described in the table overleaf along with the web address for accessing each programme. In various chapters we recommend particular programmes that can be used with groups to inform then about particular issues and to trigger discussion and planning.

Content of the DVD describing the Zanzibar Inclusive Education Programme

1. An introduction to Zanzibar Association of People with Developmental Disabilities (ZAPDD) (10 minutes)

As a key partner in the IE programme this programme introduces viewers to the background and functions of ZAPDD.
http://www.youtube.com/watch?v=JBDKRaiWiNU

2. The Foundations of IE in Zanzibar (15 minutes)

Gives an overview of the key aspects of the IE Programme. It is intended to be used as a stand alone programme for publicity about Inclusive Education.
http://www.youtube.com/watch?v=6U9vof-W1Hk

3. Working in Partnership (12 minutes)

Introduces the partners and outlines the different contributions they can make to Inclusive Education.
http://www.youtube.com/watch?v=HwqHQA2uhgI

4. Support for teachers (12 minutes)

Summarises the support provided to teachers including the role of the IE Unit in the Ministry and the provision of in-service training courses for teachers.
http://www.youtube.com/watch?v=nQ3ME787vgo

5. Organising classrooms and model lessons (30 minutes)

This programme illustrates how classrooms can be better organised to suit the needs of inclusive learners. A series of five model lessons then follow (each around 5 minutes) which are self-contained illustrations of teachers adapting a lesson to meet the needs of certain learners.
http://www.youtube.com/watch?v=RASPPdqw648

6. Skills training for youth (12 minutes)

This stand-alone programme describes the work undertaken as part of the Youth Development Programme within schools and outside of schools for youth with special needs. It challenges schools and teachers to consider the curriculum for students who cannot cope with the academic work in secondary schools but who still need education if their life chances are to be improved.
https://www.youtube.com/watch?v=yoZhVP3tKL4

Note on terminology

Throughout the book we use the terms 'learners with special needs' and 'learners with disabilities' inter-changeably to emphasise that the same strategies can apply to children and youth who require additional support even though they have no obvious impairments. Nonetheless our primary focus in on learners with physical, sensorial, cognitive and emotional impairments.

CHAPTER 1:
Planning for Inclusive Education

This chapter presents the overall strategy for promoting inclusive education based on our experiences in low-income countries. Subsequent chapters will explore each element of the strategy in greater detail but it is important that readers have an appreciation of the broader context to which they are contributing and the outcomes they are incrementally working to achieve. The chapter also examines the concept of social capital that is fundamental to the approach promoted in the book and describes the changes required in administrative systems to support inclusive schooling. A final section outlines how the book might be used within training events for teachers, families and other stakeholders.

The content of this chapter is particularly relevant to national policy-makers in education especially but also in allied Ministries. Other pertinent personnel are teacher educators, school inspectors and head teachers. Much has been written around the rationale, theory and experiences of inclusive education. Interested readers are directed to sources of further information as it is not our intention to repeat these arguments here. Rather we aim to provide a succinct overview of salient issues within three main phases of initiating inclusive education; advancing inclusive education and the desired outcomes from inclusive education. We identify how they interconnect with one another as summarised in the Figure overleaf.

The Foundations of Inclusive Education

Inclusive education is rooted within the concepts of Human Rights as expressed by the United Nations Convention of the Rights of the Child (1989) and of the Rights of Persons with Disabilities (2006) – see Chapter 2. Although many countries have ratified these Conventions, few have incorporated them into national legislation as a means of ensuring that the rights of citizens are protected, especially those who are most vulnerable in society such as children and people with disabilities. However, some governments have issued policy guidance as to how services are expected to respond to the needs of children and families; for example, how schools should address the needs of the learners with special needs.

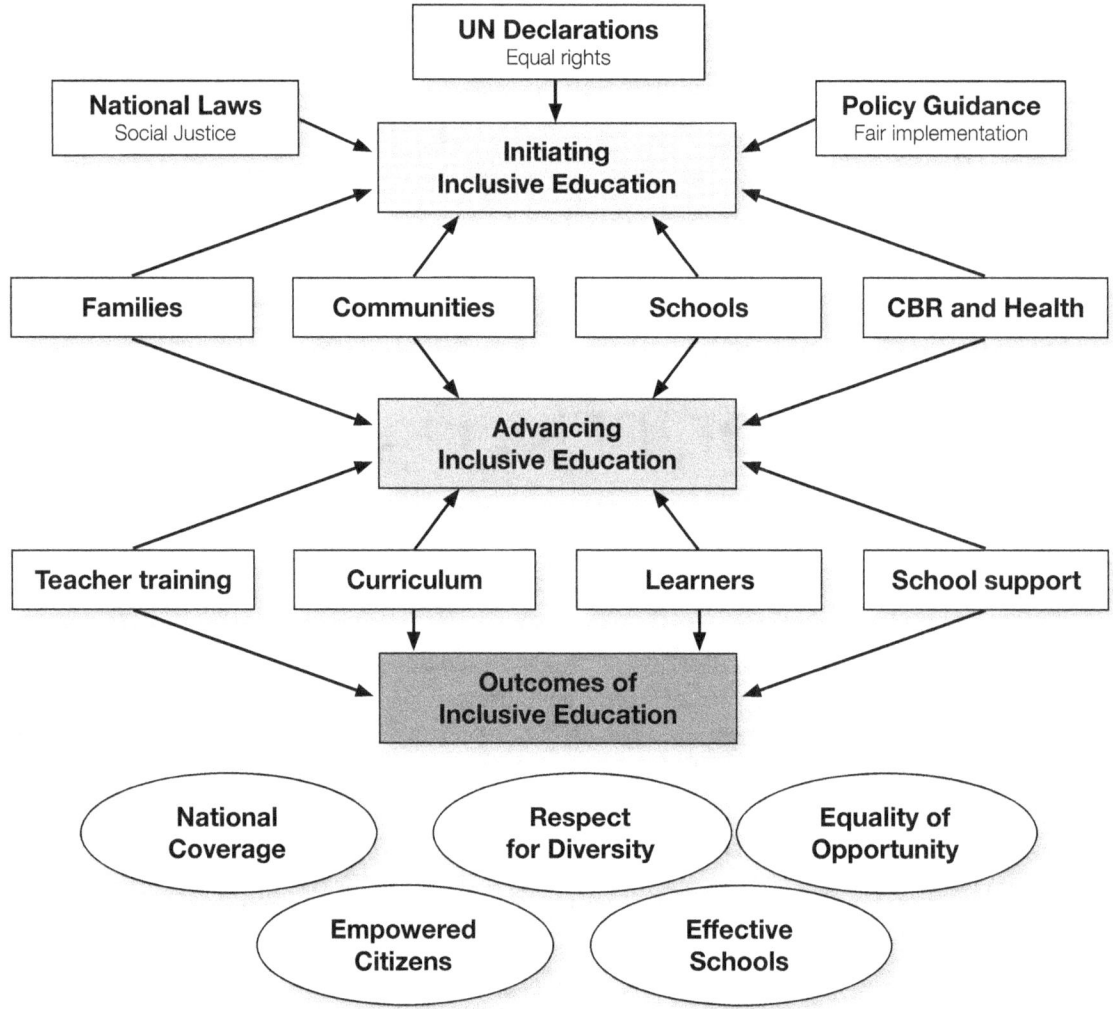

FIGURE 1: The processes influencing the development, advancement and outcomes of inclusive education
Source: McConkey & Bradley, 2010

Governments may sign international conventions of rights and yet do little to ensure their implementation in national legislation or policy guidance. Hence advocacy campaigns are often needed to make change happen. Politicians have responded to the demands of disabled person's organisations and parent associations allied with advice of professionals and community leaders. Indeed change often has to start at a local level in order to build momentum for national changes. Hence the grassroots should not wait until national laws and policies are in place, but rather they must work together towards creating the demand that will result in national changes.

Local realities

Nonetheless, the implementation of inclusive education is very much dependent on practical considerations such as the locality covered and the resources available there. This includes people, materials and finances as well as cultural factors and attitudes.

The barriers also need to be recognised. Those commonly experienced internationally are:

- The stigma and shame associated with disability that still persists in many cultures, communities and countries.

- The negative attitudes of some parents arising from having a child with disabilities. They may feel it is not worth investing in education for a disabled child.

- The negative perceptions of professionals and policy makers. They too may feel that disabled children cannot learn; they will hold back other children in the class and that scarce money would be better spent on more able children who could contribute to society.

- Protection of professional interests. Teachers may feel that having disabled children in school would mean too much extra work for them and may show up their lack of expertise as teachers. Equally teachers working in special schools may feel their jobs and work routines are threatened by placing children in ordinary schools.

- Officials with limited knowledge of educating children with disabilities who wish to run the show or being given responsibility by others for doing so. They are unable to provide the necessary leadership and things can start to fall apart.

- Various people – parents, teachers, politicians - making unconstructive criticisms which threatens the morale of those who are doing their best to make progress.

- Limited resources allied with insufficient preparation and inadequate planning.

- A lack of political will to make changes to existing systems.

Creating inclusive schools is not an easy option. All the barriers listed are real threats to this endeavour. But the message we want to emphasise is that they can be overcome; perhaps not easily nor quickly but this book will give you the ways and means for managing these challenges.

Key strategies

Figure 2 lists the key factors that contribute to greater inclusion for children with disabilities in schools. Throughout there is a strong focus on community solidarity and social responsibility.

- Orientation training for all the main stake holders. This aims to promote positive attitudes among participants, develop their knowledge and understanding, and equip them with the skills needed to make inclusion a reality.

- Expanding access to the provision of education to all learners through the successful development of 'full service' or inclusive schools that serve as a model for other schools.

- Focusing on curriculum development and assessment of learners.

- The provision of human resources, materials and finances to support schools.

- Conducting national advocacy and information campaigns and reorientation to inclusive education to other ministries.

- Revising existing policies and legislation for all levels of education.

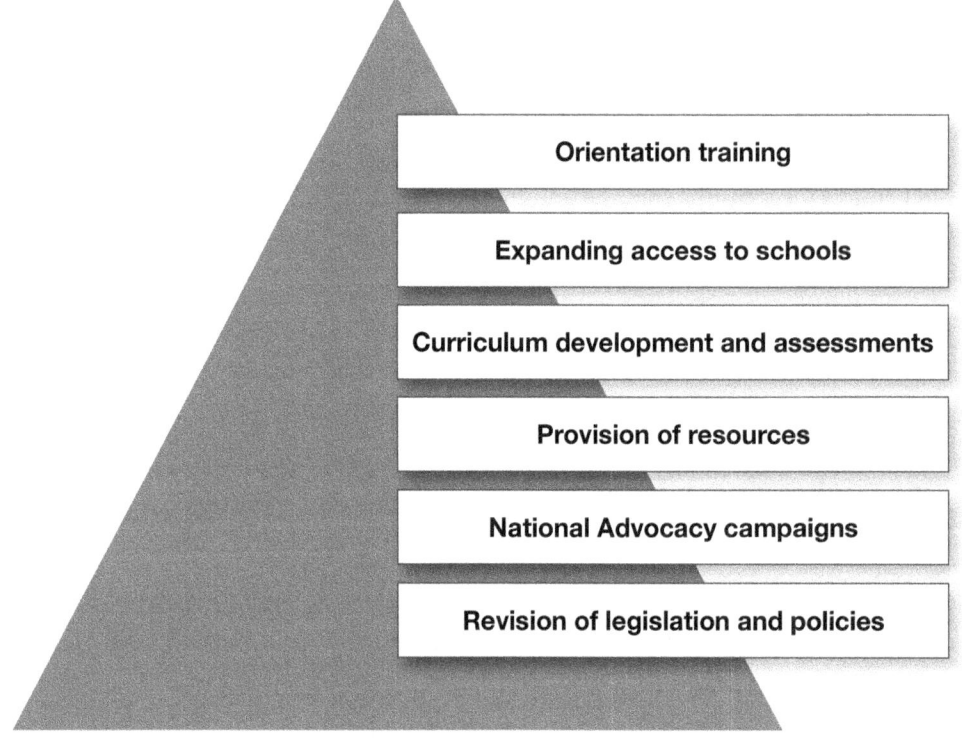

FIGURE 2: Key strategies for inclusive education

Who should be involved?

Inclusive education is not solely the responsibility of schools. This cannot be over emphasised because inclusion requires a participatory approach within communities if it is to succeed. Many groups have – or should have – a vested interest in inclusive education. The list of interested parties can be very long. From experiences of the strategies used in Lesotho, Tanzania and Zanzibar, it has to include parents and other family members, community personnel, teachers and school staff, government officials, NGOs, DPOs, professionals in education and health, social welfare and employment sectors.

The success of inclusive education in the above-mentioned countries despite their limited resources, came about because the governments were committed and had the will to start even on a small-scale. Initially Lesotho had a policy of inclusion but not the resources to implement it. Tanzania and Zanzibar developed the policy later after the pilot phases of inclusion proved that even with limited resources the results were good. In all three countries, parent organisations played a very important role in the start-up of the pilot projects, in sensitisation of other community members, in advocating for their rights and those of their children, and in lobbying politicians and officials for inclusive policies.

Elements that feature strongly

Inclusive education is a process; it is concerned with the identification and removal of barriers to children's learning. Inclusive education is about the presence, participation, and achievement of the learner in a regular class and places emphasis on learners facing difficulties or those who are marginalised or excluded.

What is good and beneficial about inclusive education is the reduction of barriers that inhibit the learning of many more children and not just those with obvious disabilities; for example, the development of an accessible and barrier free physical environment and provision of adapted learning materials and teaching strategies in schools.

Inclusion provides a focus for inter-sectorial development at local, provincial and national levels. It encourages capacity building of parents, teachers and community members. It promotes the participation of policy makers and other stakeholders in changing societal attitudes, building consensus, and mobilising changes to achieve quality education and improvements to community resources and the environment.

What contributes to the success of the inclusive education?

Our experiences, allied with those of others, suggest that the following features contribute to making inclusive education successful.

- Having leaders who are committed and knowledgeable about inclusive education at different levels. For example, local leaders can inspire local communities to meet the challenges posed by inclusion. National leaders can lobby politicians and officials in various Ministries and play an important role in changing policy and making inclusive schooling sustainable.

- Clarity of the purpose from the outset. It is vital that implementers of the process are able to defend the values, rationale and practices of inclusive education.

- Setting realistic goals and maintaining motivation on the part of all players in inclusive education is important so that results are achieved and progress is visible.

- Developing clear and manageable systems such as individual education plans, curriculum guidelines and training strategies.

- Building trust with parents and gaining their active participation through regular and good communication.

- Each school or center of learning needs to have a supportive network of interested and committed persons comprising teachers, school pupils, parents, community members and Community-Based Rehabilitation (CBR) workers and health personnel. We have called these 'Inclusive Education Committees'.

- Having a core group of personnel within the Ministry of Education – an 'Inclusive Education Unit' - with the remit to promote inclusive education and provide schools with the resources and training required to make it happen.

- Most importantly, it is imperative to have a 'hands-on' person on the ground who is visible to the community, parents, schools and the learners. Such a person needs to be able to bridge the communication gap effectively between international conventions, technical development and applying the principles to the local context. For example, an official within the Ministry with previous experience as a successful head-teacher of an inclusive school or who can provide the necessary leadership to Inclusive Education Unit.

- Finally, it is essential to undertake monitoring and evaluation of the inclusion initiatives so that successes can be identified and lessons learnt as to how strategies can be improved.

Creating Social Capital

Inclusive education is not an end to itself but rather a means to an end, namely creating a better quality of life for children and their families beyond schools and in nurturing a more equitable and just society for all (McConkey and Bradley, 2010). To do this requires what has been termed 'social capital'. The World Bank (1998) explained it in these terms:

> 'Social capital ... is not simply the sum of institutions which underpin society, it is also the glue that holds them together. It includes the shared values and rules for social conduct expressed in personal relationships, trust, and a common sense of "civic" responsibility, that makes society more than just a collection of individuals.' (p. iii)

The building of social capital is arguably crucial to an endeavour whose ultimate aim is to construct an inclusive society. Sadly this dimension to inclusive education has been undervalued to date within affluent countries and this may account for mixed results, in making this aspiration a reality. Creating social capital requires change in attitudes among stakeholders and motivation to adopt more inclusive approaches throughout the whole society and not just at the school level.

The participation of different groups in society such as parents, professionals, educational stakeholders, and the wider community such as religious groups and local politicians to name but a few, is of great importance in creating social capital. These are persons who are concerned or involved in inclusion in all its forms. That being the case, it becomes imperative that the key action is the development of clear inclusive policies that include all stakeholders and ones which are understood and accepted at the school level and in the wider community.

Putnam (2000) described how social capital can be accumulated through the processes of bonding, bridging and linking persons and communities to create greater social cohesion.

Social capital requires the **bonding** of people in communities through increasing the ties that bind people together within families or groups with common interests. These bonds give people a shared sense of identity and purpose: they build common understanding and provide mutual support to one another.

Bridging social capital covers the connections that are made across different groups within society which provide access to a wider range of formal and informal resources. Schools will be impoverished without such links and remain isolated from potential sources of support.

Linking is a third component that involves creating alliances with decision-makers and people in positions of power. This is important because disability issues are not a priority for most governments in low-income countries faced as they are with many other problems of unemployment, poverty, HIV and AIDS, and housing shortages. Likewise in times of economic stringency, strong advocacy will be required to make inclusion a priority and this need to be done at a personal, face to face level.

The inclusion strategies implemented by Mariga and her colleagues in three low-income countries exploited and promoted the approach of building social capacity through bonding, bridging, and linking (McConkey and Mariga, 2010). It is noteworthy that those links went beyond changes in school systems that have become a dominant focus of inclusive education in many affluent countries. Rather the aim was more strategic in bridging the school into local communities and wider society and joining them together in making inclusion also their responsibility..

The educational outcomes that are built on social capital are potentially far greater than the education of individual children. Of particular importance are the outcomes to be achieved by an inclusive educational system as a whole. These may be described at various levels but nationally these could be summarised as:

- National coverage of education is achieved.

- Equality of opportunities for all citizens with respect for diversity.

- Creating empowered citizens who can contribute to the local community and wider society.

- Producing effective schools for present and future generations.

Thus inclusion is not just to give particular children a better education. Rather it recognises that education is a force for social change and in creating a more equitable society in which people with disabilities and other vulnerable groups can become full and active members.

Social capital theory, however, has its critics. It overlooks the selfishness of human nature and the competitive element that inhibits cooperation. Little attention has been paid to how social capital can be grown particularly in autocratic societies and systems. Nevertheless, the concept of building social capital does seem to provide a framework for how schools might become more closely connected into their communities through building bridges and linkages with significant individuals and groups.

However, the starting point is the same for each – relationships need to be built between these individuals and schools. This might start with one or two interested persons from the group but through them understandings can develop as to how each can help another. It may not be possible to generate an interest across all societal groups, but you can start with those with whom you already have some contact or those that appear most interested.

IDEAS FOR COMMUNICATING THE MESSAGES

- Identify the groups within the community who could be supporters of inclusive education.
- What are the advantages of schools working more closely with community groups and organisations?

Administrative Structures to Support Inclusion

Change has to embrace the wider educational system as well as schools. An inclusive education policy has particular implications for special schools.

Implications for special schools

A favoured solution in nearly all countries has been to provide special schools for 'different children' and usually for pupils with specific disabilities such as hearing impairment, visual impairment and intellectual disabilities. Often these schools were begun by voluntary and religious organisations in response to needs in a particular locality. Experience has taught us that this approach can mean that many children with disabilities in less affluent countries get no education at all (Peters, 2004). Among the reasons are:

- Special schools are a high-cost option which many poorer countries, who struggle even to provide educational access for non-disabled children, cannot afford.

- Special schools tend to be located in urban centres and serve more affluent families who can afford the fees, whereas the majority of needy children live in rural areas.

- It is not viable in rural areas to provide special schools for all the different impairments that children may experience.

- The expertise of specialist teachers based in special schools is not shared with teachers in mainstream schools, who have few opportunities to learn how best to teach children with difficulties in learning.

Equally, the value of providing special schools in more affluent countries is questioned for these and other reasons (Ainscow, 1991):

- Inclusive schools provide children with more educational and social opportunities than they receive in special schools.

- Parents increasingly opt to send their children to mainstream schools as special schools can stigmatise them.

- Disabled activists have been critical of the education they received in special schools and argue that it sustains discriminatory attitudes within society (albeit with the best of intentions).

UNESCO organised a World Conference on Special Needs Education in 1994; held in Salamanca, Spain. The final report concluded that children with special educational needs must have access to ordinary schools. They argued that:

> Regular schools with this inclusive orientation are the most effective means of combating discriminatory attitudes, creating welcoming communities, building an inclusive society and achieving education for all. Moreover, they provide an effective education to the majority of children and improve the efficiency and ultimately the cost-effectiveness of the entire education system. (UNESCO, 1994, p.10)

At that time, the UNESCO statement recognised that certain children may best be taught in special classes or schools because of their particular needs in communication, such as pupils who are deaf, deaf-blind or severely intellectually disabled. Latterly, experience has shown that these learners can be placed in mainstream schools although many countries provide Special Units for them.

But inclusive education is not achieved simply by incorporating these children into primary-school classes. Rather, teachers, schools and educational systems need to change so that they can better accommodate the diversity of pupils' needs and ensure that children with disabilities are included in all aspects of school life. It also means identifying the physical and social barriers within and around the school that hinder learning and actively seeking to reduce or remove these barriers. Thus inclusive education means transforming how schools presently function. These changes stand to benefit all learners and make the whole education system more cost effective.

New administrative structures

The successful formulation, implementation and sustenance of inclusive education depends on effective and informed administrative systems within the education system. Existing systems were designed to support segratated schooling so these may need to be created or modified to manage the transition to inclusive education. As a start, personnel involved in education management at all tiers of governance should attend orientation workshops on ways to accommodate diversity and provide support for all learners and management skills in order to facilitate this. This will need to embrace pre-primary, primary and secondary education. School inspectors and staff in advisory roles should also participate. Also there is a need to focus on building capacity of managers and staff in institutions of higher education with responsibility for teacher education.

The Minister or the Ministry of Education has the political responsibility for transforming the education system. This could be facilitated by setting up the required working committees and regulatory frameworks to respond to the specific issues accommodating diversity and addressing barriers or limitations to learning and necessary development to be achieved.

International opinion warns against building special education infrastructures within the Ministry of Education. This leads to a parallel administration for special education where disabled and vulnerable children are excluded from the ordinary or regular education system. Nonetheless there is a need to have a cadre of staff who have experience of teaching pupils with disabilities who can provide leadership and training for all schools.

The Ministry will need to provide a policy document that outlines the approach to Inclusive Education that is proposed. This will work towards transformation of the education system as a whole in the following key areas:

- Facilitating of access to education including community initiatives.
- The development of a single education system that will cater for all learners needs.
- Supporting all stakeholders, i.e. parents, teachers, students and the community at large in achieving inclusive schools.
- Building a relevant research agenda to inform present and future policy and legislation.

Leadership for inclusion

Within educational systems champions are needed to provide the leadership required to make inclusive education successful. In our experience, these are some of qualities required of leaders.

- Grassroots experience of working with children and families.
- Experience of teaching and trained in special education.
- Knowledge of community development strategies and familiarity with health and social service systems.

- Committed and passionate about inclusion; prepared to work long hours.
- Humble and prepared to listen to the opinions and concerns of others.
- Able communicators who can convey complex ideas to a range of audiences.
- A team player who can motivate others and prepared to delegate tasks and responsibilities.
- Capable of planning ahead, well-organised and able to manage a variety of tasks.

It is rare to find all of these qualities in the one person, so often a project team may need to be formed to take forward the implementation of inclusive education. In Lesotho and Zanzibar a small group of teachers were seconded to the Ministry of Education to work under the combined leadership of Lilian Mariga and a local colleague. They were based within the Primary Education section of the Ministry. In some instances the persons chosen had were sent for further training to equip them for their new role.

Funds for inclusion

Sources of funding for inclusion need to be identified. This may mean using existing funding more effectively. However the funding allocated for the education for learners with 'special needs' and education support services is often inadequate and reflects disparities and inequalities in the way fiscal resources are allocated and distributed. Even when money is available, it is mostly directed towards the specialised schools and units. Little funding has been directed towards addressing special needs of pupils in the overall system and to breaking down existing barriers to their learning and development. Increasingly financial constraints are exacerbated by inefficiencies in the way in which educational funding as a whole is managed and organised, the areas of priority expenditure which are targeted and general functioning of the education system as a whole.

Unfortunately, inclusive education cannot be a quick fix. It requires a change in long established national systems and that requires much effort. Inclusive education requires adjustments to the attitudes and practices of family, communities and other systems such as health services and community work. These will incur extra start-up costs. For example, specific programmes or activities may have to be run involving diverse groups in promoting inclusive education and funding has to be found to do this. These might encompass the following: the formation of a parent organisation, empowering parents through information and training, parent participation in assessment and the preparation of individual education plans and developing a strong movement to advocate and lobby for inclusive policies and budgets. Moreover change challenges the vested interest of powerful groups in education who can slow down and even stop the necessary changes.

The transformations identified for schools need not stop there. New forms of ' learning centres' may need to be established outside of the educational systems to provide particular forms of education and training according to pupils' needs and interests - for an example artisan schools, vocational centres and creative arts venues – particularly for teenagers and young adults who would benefit from a different curriculum to that traditionally provided in schools. Once again the lack of funding can inhibit such developments.

In Lesotho, Zanzibar and Tanzania, international donors covered some of the start-up costs of inclusive education. In association with UNICEF, Save the Children (UK) provided technical support over a six-year period to the Ministry of Education in Lesotho. This covered the costs of a national advisor (Lilian Mariga) plus additional training, resource and evaluation costs. In Tanzania and Zanzibar, the Norwegian Association for Persons with Developmental Disabilities (NFU) with funds from Operation Days Work (ODW) supported the Ministry of Education and Vocational Training in undertaking feasibility, piloting and evaluation of inclusive education. These monies were channelled through the national parent associations for persons with intellectual disabilities and covered Mariga's consultancy costs, the development and production of training materials, and the provision of training courses. The government sourced support from other international agencies until the costs could be included in the national education budget.

Success in accessing monies for inclusive schooling came from educating policy makers on the importance of this initiative to the goal of improving basic or primary education. A second step is a commitment to a step-wise process for replacing initial donor money with mainstream government funding; starting from say a 20% investment in year 1 and rising by 20% per year until 100% funding is achieved. Experience from the three African programmes showed that this took at least four years. Thirdly, successful pilots in local schools clearly demonstrated the outcomes from inclusion. These helped to convince the top policy-makers to invest in these programmes.

Final thoughts

This chapter has presented an overview of the various considerations to be borne in mind when developing an inclusive education strategy within low-income countries in particular. It is written mainly as a background briefing for persons who may take on a training function. However, the content can also be shared with policy makers across Government and particularly politicians.

CHAPTER 2:
Introducing Inclusive Education

Inclusive education is a new concept in many countries. Previously children who were different were excluded from schools or else they attended special schools. This means that many teachers and pupils have not had the experience of sharing their schools with children who are disabled. But If we are to respect the rights of all children, then national educational systems must be inclusive; "actively seeking out children who are not enrolled, and responding flexibly to the circumstances and needs of all learners" (Dakar Framework for Action, 2000). This Unit gives an overview of what the development of inclusive education means in the broadest sense and the international support that underpins it. We examine where inclusive education is heading in some southern countries with very limited resources. The chapter provides information on holistic and practical perspectives on how school and classrooms can become more inclusive and 'learner' friendly. It builds on experiences gained over the years and on strategies and tools developed by many sectors dealing with and working in inclusive education.

The content of the chapter can provide the basis for training inputs that aim to introduce the concept of Inclusive Education to various stake-holder groups. Four main themes are reviewed but not all of these may need to be covered in the training for certain groups.

Key Learning Messages

Training inputs on this theme aim to inspire participants to become actively involved in promoting and developing inclusive schools within their community. The main learning objectives are for them to:

– Understand the meaning of inclusive education.

– Appreciate the international declarations and training materials that support inclusion.

– Describe the prerequisites for making inclusive education possible.

– To summarise the benefits of inclusive schools.

Rationale for the training

Giving participants a clear understanding of inclusive education is very important. Different underlying principles and values can produce different outcomes. Inclusive education will fail or be unsuitable when a limited definition or one based on the assumption that 'the-children-is-a-problem' is used to develop or monitor practice.

However, the definition of inclusive education must continue evolving if inclusive education is to remain a real and valuable response to addressing educational human rights challenges.

Inclusion and inclusive education is not another name for special education needs. It involves a different approach to identifying and attempting to resolve difficulties that arise in schools. Rather it is a process of addressing and responding to the diversity needs for all learners through increasing participation in learning, in cultural activities and in communities and reducing exclusion within and from education. It involves changes and modification of content, approaches, structures and strategies with a common vision that covers all children of the appropriate age range and the conviction that it is the responsibility of the regular system to educate all children.

Inclusive education and the right of all learners to a quality education

Inclusive education is a dynamic approach of responding positively to pupils with diversity and seeing individual differences not as a problem but as an opportunity for enriching learning. Inclusive education involves the processes of increasing the participation of pupils in, and reducing their exclusion from cultures, curricula and communities of the school. Its aim is to eliminate exclusion that is a consequence of negative attitudes. Inclusive education has evolved as a movement to challenge exclusionary policies and practices. It is the responsibility of both the formal and informal sectors.

Inclusive education further involves restructuring of cultures, policies and practices to respond to the diversity of students in their localities. It improves learning and participatory process of all students including those vulnerable to exclusionary pressures. This includes not only children with disabilities but others who risk exclusion because of ethnicity, gender and poverty. Inclusive education helps to overcome barriers to access and participation. It promotes the rights of students to learn in their own community schools, strengthens relationships between schools and their communities and accepts that schooling is an essential component of inclusive communities.

Inclusive education is also about improving schools. It involves transforming schools and their context of learning so that they truly cater for all children. It means improving schools for the staff as well as for students.

Key concepts underpinning inclusive education

Perhaps a good starting point is not to focus on inclusive schools but rather to invite people to think about their values and beliefs with respect to children, community and society. From this analysis they will begin to appreciate that inclusion proves a means for fulfilling their ambitions. Listed below are questions you might invite participants in training courses to ponder.

- **Concepts about learners:** Are children of the same age all like one another – for example five year olds coming to school for the first time; or 11 year olds moving into adolescence? Are all children capable of learning, even if some are slower than others? Can children who have difficulties in learning be helped to learn? Should all children have the right to education within their own community?

- **Concepts about education:** When do children start learning and who first helps them to learn? What would make schools a place that children enjoy going to each day? What could teachers do to help children who have difficulties in keeping up with the other children in the class? How could the local community and parents in particular, support their local schools?

- **Concepts about community:** Are people with disabilities treated fairly in your community? As a parent of non-disabled child, how would you feel if told your child cannot attend the local school – what would you do about it? Why do children bully other children who are seen as different – call them names, assault them?

These questions and others like them, should help people to become more aware of the key drivers for the international emphasis that exists for inclusive schools. In summary, they are:

- All children have the right to education.

- Local schools are best placed to make this right a reality.

- Schools need to remove the barriers that currently exist to pupils' learning in schools. Teaching should be flexible and responsive to pupil needs and abilities.
- Education is broader than formal schooling. Schools need the support of families and community.
- Inclusion builds stronger communities that respect diversity and removes discrimination.
- Inclusion encourages inter-sector and partnership working. It results in better use of scarce resources.
- An emphasis on inclusion can empower local people to take ownership and responsibility for improving their community.

The main themes in introducing Inclusive Education

We have identified four main themes that could be covered in introducing participants to Inclusive Education. For each theme we provide background information that could be share with participants and suggest some activities that could be used to do this.

Theme 1: Defining Inclusive Education

Inclusive education refers to the right of all children to attend school in their home community in ordinary/regular classes with peers of their own age. All children have a right to quality and meaningful education. This means including children who are usually left out. Here our focus is mostly on children with disabilities, such as children with difficulties in seeing and the few who are totally blind; those who have hearing difficulties and those who are totally deaf, those who cannot walk or have problems using their arms and hands, those who are slow in learning, those who have difficulties communicating and others who have chronic illnesses or conditions such as epilepsy. There will also be some pupils who have more than one impairment.

But these children are frequently disadvantaged in other ways; most of all by poverty but they may also be children of immigrants or ethnic minorities or simply female and viewed as not needing to be educated - all of which increases their risk of exclusion beyond that of their disability.

Inclusive education acknowledges that all children can learn and that all pupils – including many considered to be non-disabled - need some form of support in learning during their time at school. Inclusive education aims to uncover and minimise barriers to learning. It is broader than formal schooling and includes the home and the community. Hence it is about changing attitudes, behaviours, teaching methods, curricula and environment to meet the needs of all children. In fact inclusion is a dynamic process which is constantly evolving according to local cultures and contexts and is part of the wider strategy to promote an inclusive society.

The topic of inclusive education cannot be well understood without defining the meaning of other terms and approaches. We focus on three: special education, integration and special units. These different terms reflect the historical development of inclusive education particularly in the countries of the north. On the other hand, these approaches are still being implemented and promoted in many countries and yet the differences between them and inclusive education remains poorly understood. Admittedly these terms have positive concepts in common in relation to the education of students with disabilities but there are important differences between special education and inclusive education.

Special Education

Special education assumes that there is a separate group of children who have 'special educational needs' and are often called 'special needs children'. This assumption is not valid because any child can experience difficulty in learning. Many disabled children have no problem with learning, only in access to suitable teaching and learning opportunities, yet they are still labelled 'special needs' children. Most children want to learn when given the appropriate environment and encouragement. It is now clear that children with severe intellectual impairments can also learn very well in certain areas or at certain stages of their life, if their needs are recognised and if the right teaching methods are used.

Special education is often seen as an alternative to ordinary schooling which acts as separate supplement to general education provision. Hence in many countries, special education has evolved into an entirely separate education system. But recently this has been challenged both from a human rights perspective and from the point of view of effectiveness. In fact, special education systems often do not define the term 'special' and in reality what is often called 'special' is in fact an ordinary learning need (Stubbs, 2008).

Special education sees the child as the problem, not the system or the teacher. It defines the whole child solely on the basis of his/her impairment and segregates them on this basis. Hence there may be separate schools for children with physical and intellectual disabilities, for pupils with hearing impairments and for those with vision loss. Special education further defines the child on the basis of impairment or disability. Yet the majority of children with disability or impairments have the same characteristics and qualities as any child. It aspires to correct the child's perceived deficits and problems rather than respecting and building up her/his own strengths and working round their limitations.

Integrated Education

The term is commonly used to describe the process of bringing children with disabilities into an ordinary school but focusing on the individual child fitting into the existing school system and doing little to adjust the system. In some countries this is known as mainstreaming. The child is seen as a problem and must be prepared for integration rather than the school being ready. Often children are moved or accepted into school and is of little concern whether the child is learning or not. The focus is on the individual child and not the teachers' skills or the system. In these circumstances many children drop out or repeat classes for many years. The majority of the extra resources and methods (if available at all) are focused on the individual child and not on the teachers' skills and system.

Integration sometimes just refers to a geographical process – moving a child physically into mainstream school. It ignores issues whether the child is really being accepted and included. It also fails to consider what changes are needed in the curriculum or in the organisation of the school to ensure that it is accessible to the range of diversity of all its students.

When the child drops out, repeats many years, or is excluded then this is perceived to be the child's fault, or that he/she could not follow the curriculum, or they could not walk to school, or that they could not cope with other children's comments.

Integration often focuses on a group of pupils especially those with specific learning difficulties such as dyslexia. It has been easier to integrate these children into ordinary schools than it has been with children who have more significant disabilities. Even so, the integrated child in most cases is left to cope with a rigid mainstreaming system that is based on the same concept as special education.

Special Units

The term is used to mean a special classroom or building, generally with a special teacher solely for children with special educational needs. Because the unit or building is attached to a regular school, they often use the term inclusive education, but in reality it can easily become a segregated classroom. It is based on the same philosophy as special schools. This practice promotes exclusion and is therefore a strategy to avoid.

The mainstream teachers think it is the 'special' teachers' responsibility to deal with a child who is experiencing learning difficulties. They often resent having a high number of pupils in their classes compared to those in the units. Children are often labelled as a special needs group. In some instances children with different impairments are lumped together in those Units based on the same arbitrary characteristics rather than an actual need. There is often no specific learning advantage in grouping them like this. Instead stigma and separation are perpetuated. Small units do not foster team-teaching or a whole school approach. Instead they erroneously reinforce the idea that teachers with special techniques are needed to resolve children's learning problems.

That said, special units are commonly used for to provide a more inclusive education for children with more severe impairments. However they function best in this regard if children graduate from the unit and take their place in regular classes or when pupils attend the unit for certain subjects but spend most of the time with their non-disabled peers.

Inclusive Education

As noted previously, inclusive education is based on the following basic concepts that participants need to understand:

- The right of all children including children with disabilities to education.

- A commitment to finding methods to help children who function in a different way and at different speeds of learning.

- Promoting and developing the child's potential in a holistic way: physical, linguistic, social, cognitive and sensory.
- Supporting different methods of communication with a range of impairments.
- Key players in special needs education are parents, teachers, communities, school authorities, policy makers, curriculum planners, training institutes and people with disabilities.
- Above all, Inclusion means changing the educational system to suit the children.

People will often argue that children with severe disabilities cannot be taught in ordinary classrooms. This is a very good example of how education systems need to change. Education in its true sense does not mean only reading and writing. For learners with severe disabilities, it means being equipped with functional skills that enables them to be part of the family and community. For the severely disabled, inclusion and recognition by society is of great importance to their future life as citizens of their local community.

In fact, throughout history and across cultures, there are many forms of education based on particular philosophies, spiritual and religious beliefs or systems. One tradition uses non-formal approaches and is often relevant, practical, and flexible, oriented to local cultures and people, and utilising local resources and personnel. Priority is given to preparation for real life; that is activities of daily living, employment and citizenship. This non-formal approach has been particularly developed in India (UNESCO, 2002). Mariga et all (1986) used these approaches in rural Africa and experience suggests that they lead to the acceptance of the persons with severe disabilities and their general inclusion.

IDEAS FOR COMMUNICATING THE MESSAGES

Ask participants to write a definition for inclusive education that would make it understandable to the following groups:

- Parents
- Children in primary schools
- Members of school committees

Theme 2: International Support for Inclusive Education

Fundamentally inclusive education is a human rights issue that is enunciated in various international instruments. In this section we list those most relevant to inclusive education and give you the web address where you can obtain copies of each one.

Children and adults with disabilities are frequently denied their fundamental right to education. This is based on the assumption that people with disabilities and other vulnerable groups do not count as full human beings, and so are seen as the exceptions in terms of universal rights.

Lobbying by parents and other disability groups has ensured that the 2007 United Nations

Convention on the Rights of Persons with Disabilities establishes in international law that all persons with disabilities - no matter how severely disabled - have a right to education.

Similarly the 1989 United Nations Convention on Rights of the Child stressed the right of ALL children to an education. These statements of Rights are instruments that most countries have signed or ratified. However the right to education does not automatically imply inclusion. Nevertheless the right to education within mainstream systems and the prohibition of discriminatory practices is highlighted in more detailed instruments such as the Jomtien Declaration (1990) and is clearly stated in the Salamanca Statement prepared by UNESCO (1994) and the associated framework for action.

Timeline and sources of international instruments relating to Inclusive Education

1948   Universal Declaration of Human Rights: http://www.un.org/en/documents/udhr/

1989   UN Convention on Rights of Children: http://www2.ohchr.org/english/law/crc.htm

1990   The World Declaration on Education for All, Jomtien:
http://www.unesco.org/education/wef/en-conf/Jomtien%20Declaration%20eng.shtm

1993   The UN Standard Rules on Equalisation of Opportunities for Disabled People:
http://www.un.org/esa/socdev/enable/dissre00.htm

1994   UNESCO: The Salamanca Statement and Framework for Action on Special Needs Education:
http://www.unesco.org/education/pdf/SALAMA_E.PDF

1999   Salamanca five year review:
http://unesdoc.unesco.org/images/0011/001181/118118eo.pdf

2000   Education Forum for Action, Dakar:
http://www.unesco.org/education/wef/en-conf/dakfram.shtm

2000   Millennium Development goals focusing on Poverty Reduction and Development:
http://www.un.org/millenniumgoals/

2004   Education For All Flagship on Education and Disability (UNESCO and University of Oslo):
http://www.unesco.org/education/efa/know_sharing/flagship_initiatives/depliant_flagship.pdf

2007   UN Convention on Rights of Persons with Disabilities:
http://www.un.org/disabilities/convention/conventionfull.shtml

International instruments

The following are some of the international instruments relevant to inclusive education.

United Nations Convention on the Rights of Persons with Disabilities

Since 1948 the United Nations has issued various Declarations of Rights culminating in 2007 in the Convention on the Rights of Persons with Disabilities (CRPD). The drafting of this

Convention was a challenging yet inspiring process. Civil society and people with disabilities in particular played a central role. Although article 24 on education elicited strong and opposing views, it commits governments to ensuring that their education systems are inclusive (Mittler, 2012).

Article 24 – Education

1. States Parties recognise the right of persons with disabilities to education. With a view to realising this right without discrimination and on the basis of equal opportunity, States Parties shall ensure an inclusive education system at all levels and life long learning directed to:

   a) The full development of human potential and sense of dignity and self-worth, and the strengthening of respect for human rights, fundamental freedoms and human diversity;

   b) The development by persons with disabilities of their personality, talents and creativity, as well as their mental and physical abilities, to their fullest potential;

   c) Enabling persons with disabilities to participate effectively in a free society.

2. In realising this right, States Parties shall ensure that:

   a) Persons with disabilities are not excluded from the general education system on the basis of disability, and that children with disabilities are not excluded from free and compulsory primary education, or from secondary education, on the basis of disability;

   b) Persons with disabilities can access an inclusive, quality and free primary education and secondary education on an equal basis with others in the communities in which they live;

   c) Reasonable accommodation of the individual's requirements is provided;

   d) Persons with disabilities receive the support required, within the general education system, to facilitate their effective education;

   e) Effective individualised support measures are provided in environments that maximise academic and social development, consistent with the goal of full inclusion.

Children with disabilities and adults are however, frequently denied this fundamental right as others are seen to have greater priority. But lobbying by the disabled groups has ensured that the recent UN Conventions make specific mention of disabled people, and emphasise that all disabled persons, no matter how severely disabled, have a right to education. Nevertheless in many African countries this right is ignored and children with the most severe disabilities are even excluded from special schools. For example, in 2010 the Government of South Africa was challenged on this policy and they were directed by the courts to ensure that education was provided to all children. Similar legal actions were used in other countries such as Ireland to bring about similar changes.

The Jomtien World Declaration on Education for all, Thailand (1990) and Dakar Framework (2000)

The Jomtien Declaration on Education for All committed World Governments to providing all the world's children with an education by 2015. It recognised that particular groups needed particular attention if this goal was to be achieved. In article 111 on "Universalizing Access and Promoting Equity", it states that very marked educational disparities existed and that many different particular groups were vulnerable to discrimination and exclusion. These include girls, street children, the poor rural and remote population, ethnic minorities and other groups with particular mention of children with disabilities. Moreover the latter also formed a significant part of those other marginalised groups such as the rural poor.

In April 2000, more than 1,100 participants from 164 countries gathered in Dakar, Senegal, for a World Education Forum to review progress in achieving Education for All. Ranging from teachers to ministers, academics to policy makers, non-governmental bodies to heads of major international organisations, they adopted a World Framework for Action (2000). The Forum collectively adopted this commitment:

> "In order to attract and retain children from being marginalised and excluded groups, education systems should respond flexibly. Education systems must be inclusive, actively seeking out children who are not enrolled, and responding flexibly to the circumstances and needs of learners".

Six goals were developed:

- Expand early childhood care and education.
- Provide free and compulsory primary education for all.
- Promote learning and life skills for adults.
- Increase adult literacy.
- Achieve gender priority by 2015.
- Improve the quality of education.

The UN Standard Rules on the Equalisation of Opportunities (1993)

The Standard Rules on Equalisation of Opportunities for Persons with Disabilities (1993) consists of rules governing all aspects of disabled person's rights. Rule six focuses on education and agrees with Jomtien that disabled persons should be educated as an integral part of the mainstream and that States should ensure they take responsibility for disabled persons' education. In many countries the education of people was provided by non-government agencies thereby letting the government off the hook. The UN standard Rule 6 stated the importance of proper resourcing for inclusion. It is recognised that there is still a long way to go before inclusion and education for all becomes a reality.

The UN Standard Rules for equal opportunities emphases that the State should take responsibility for people with disabilities and should have a clear policy, have a flexible curriculum and provide quality learning materials and an on-going teacher training. Schools should be properly resourced. Particular emphasis was placed on involving parents and disabled people's organisations and community programmes as important supports to inclusion and inclusive education.

> "Parent groups and organisations of persons with disabilities should be involved in the education process at all levels. Integrated education and community-based programmes should be seen as complementary approaches in providing cost-effective education and training for persons with disabilities. National community-based programmes should encourage communities to use and develop their resources to provide local education to persons with disabilities".

Salamanca Statement (1994)

The UNESCO Salamanca statement identified the benefits of inclusive education:

> "The merit of such schools is not only that they are capable of providing quality education to all children; their establishment is a crucial step in helping to change discriminatory attitudes , in creating welcoming communities and in developing an inclusive society. A change in social perspective is imperative. For far too long, the problems of people with disabilities have been compounded by a disabling society that has focused upon their impairments rather than their potential" (p.7).

Internationally the focus has shifted from special and segregated schools for children with disabilities. Instead local communities are deemed responsible for providing an effective education for all children. This ethos stems from the Disability Rights movement and reflects the aspirations and experience of different groups of people with disabilities. However visually impaired and deaf people in particular had often benefited from education in special schools otherwise they would have been either uneducated, or unable to access the regular curriculum within the mainstream school. This debate still continues although the main thrust of the Salamanca statement was to find ways to enable all children to be educated work together while acknowledging their diversity. Today the Salamanca Statement is the key international document on the principles and practice of inclusive education.

> IDEAS FOR COMMUNICATING THE MESSAGES
> - Obtain a copy of the latest educational policy for your country. Identify what it says about children with disabilities and their education. Invite participants to indicate if they feel the policy is being put into practice in their location.
> - What steps are needed to make local schools more inclusive?

Theme 3: Prerequisites for Inclusive Education

In this section, we summarise the main prerequisites that are required to make inclusive education a success. These will be elaborated in later chapters.

As noted previously, inclusive education is about ensuring the rights to education of all learners, regardless of their individual characteristics or difficulties, in order to build a more just society. Inclusive education is not just about schools but it is about society. The starting point is to see inclusive education as emerging from the overlapping circles of inclusion and the accompanying assets that are present in all human societies. Although we may speak of 'under-developed' countries this is often equated with narrow concepts of economic growth and we forget the vast heritage of cultural, spiritual and human development existing in these countries. The challenge is to link this inheritance to the achievement of full human rights, sustainability of resources and respect for the environment, social responsibility and celebration of diversity. Hence inclusive education is a means whereby marginalised children and adults – whatever their gender, age, ability, disability, ethnicity, religion, health or social status - can participate and contribute to the society. Inclusion circles exist in families, local neighbours, communities as well as other service organisations in health and community development. On this foundation, the task of making schools more inclusive can be built.

The main prerequisites for Inclusive Education are:

- Political will – this includes senior officials within Ministries as well as Government ministers and members of parliament.

- Empowerment of advocacy groups such as disabled people's organisations and parent associations.

- Participation of people with disabilities and their parents and communities at a local level to support schools to bring about changes.

- Policy statements, guiding principles and ideally legislation.

- Resources that is human, financial and material resources.

- An action plan with clear targets and a timetable for implementation.

Inclusive education calls for a change of attitudes in society and schools to make them responsive to the needs all children. It demands wide-ranging changes involving the whole of the education system, which cannot be taken in isolation, although this becomes especially difficult where other educational and social systems remain unreformed and exclusive. Inclusion needs to be a universal priority.

Many African countries have already started formulating inclusive policies and have begun implementing them. These policies support education for all children but because some have not specified implementation strategies and addressed budgetary matters; progress has been sporadic at best. Other countries in the transition process of developing an inclusive education provision are aware that the process does not necessarily require large amounts of new money and new resources. The key factors are for the government to:

– Redirect the existing funding towards the development of the inclusive initiatives.

– Make sure initiatives are built on existing resources, mechanisms for schools, local authorities and other sectors involved in inclusive development.

– Development aid from international donors supports Inclusive Education and NOT segregated provision.

The process of Inclusive Education

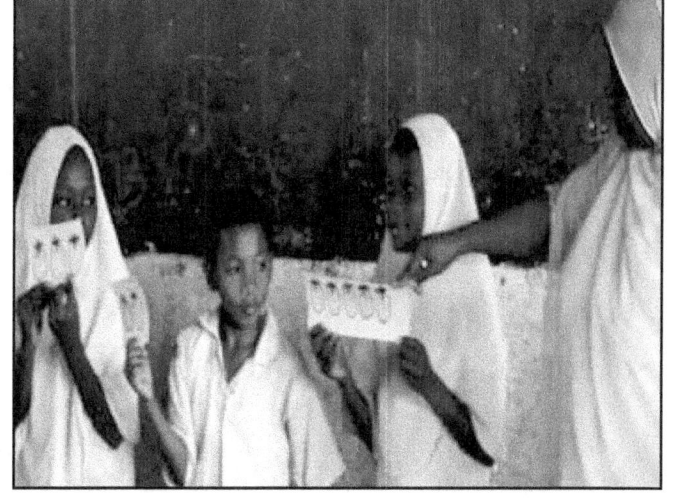

Inclusive education initiatives in Lesotho, Tanzania and Zanzibar started with feasibility studies (see Chapter 7). The initial aim was to understand cultural norms, existing resources and systems with a focus on helping teachers to respond better to the identified needs of children and families in their local community, including finding ways to make the curriculum accessible to those with impairments. But even before the feasibility studies commenced, the Ministries were prepared to make a commitment to inclusion though the resources to implement it were limited and had to be augmented by international donors.

The move to inclusive education requires a process of ongoing change based on clearly articulated set of principles and should be seen as a programme of wide-ranging development and reform. It calls for transparency through the creation of awareness on the changes needed to existing policy and legislation. It requires constant advocacy to ensure that the target group and society at large will benefit from inclusive education. It further requires mobilising opinion, building consensus, carrying out analysis of barriers encountered and gaining support from all sectors.

The change often requires systemic change in administration structures and re-educating of the stakeholders in the education system and schools. This change calls for building of partnerships, human and financial support that should have clearly articulated guiding principles allied with access to education and to physical structures and establishment of procedures and practices throughout the education system.

The development of professionals throughout the education system is crucial, notably the pre and in-service training of teachers.

Nevertheless improvement of schools in rural settings is particularly challenging where service systems can be impaired by:

- Inadequate sensitisation of community members.
- Lack of appropriate resources and appliances.
- Lack of transport and poor road conditions.
- Inaccessible systems and physical facilities.
- Negative attitudes coupled by unfounded beliefs.

In sum, there can be formidable barriers to making educational systems more inclusive. Identifying the prerequisites is the beginning of a realistic appraisal of the work to be done and who is best placed to lead and guide the programme of change and reform that is required.

> **IDEAS FOR COMMUNICATING THE MESSAGES**
>
> Show programme 1 from Video series – *Inclusion in Action* (Zanzibar). This illustrates the different prerequisites that were put in place as a means of introducing Inclusive Education into Zanzibar.

Theme 4: The Benefits of Inclusion Education

Despite the previously mentioned hurdles, there are many perceived benefits of inclusion and inclusive education. As a catalyst for change, inclusive education not only provides school improvement for all learners and teachers but leads to an increase in awareness of human rights and a reduction of discrimination. Through finding local solutions to the complex problem of inclusion, it promotes an inclusive society and inclusive development. At a personal level it promotes a better understanding of disability at an early stage and prepares the child for inclusion in a school setting. It promotes the need for children to feel safe and secured. All children need a close, sensitive and loving relationship with adults who care for them. It is the basis for the development of the child's sense of security, confidence and ability to cope well with other people and the world at large.

In summary, the main benefits are:

- Inclusive education acknowledges that all children can learn and it respects differences in children based on age, gender, ethnicity, language and disabilities.

- It enables the disadvantaged and persons with disabilities to develop their potential, and contribute to society and be enriched by their difference and not devalued as a result.
- Inclusive education offers learners and their families practical skills and knowledge needed to breakout the circle of poverty in which many are trapped.
- Inclusive education enables children with disabilities and other vulnerable groups to stay with their families and attend their neighborhoods regular schools without sending the children to an institution which is against their rights.
- Inclusive education benefits the whole school including the staff.
- All pupils in schools gain when teachers adapt the curricula and teaching method.
- When teachers take on the challenge of making their classrooms and schools more inclusive, they become more skilful and better practitioners. Teachers found they profited greatly from the process:

> "I now enjoy teaching more. The programme helped us with different teaching techniques for the so-called normal pupils; even after hours we stay to prepare to cope with individual differences. I found that having knowledge of assessing strengths and weaknesses helps me to understand the students' needs individually."

- Teachers are not the sole players in making inclusive education a reality. Other key players are medical teams, therapists, counsellors, social workers, parents and other community members. It increases a sense of team-working and partnership as other circles of inclusion are created.
- The budget will be high at the beginning but as the system becomes well established it costs not much extra as it would when persons with disabilities are placed in institutions or special schools.
- Inclusion promotes change of negative attitudes and brings about acceptance of people with disabilities and the disadvantaged.
- It promotes the inclusion of disabled and disadvantaged people in all matters affecting their lives and those of local communities.

A key message is that everyone stands to benefit from inclusion – there are only winners, no losers! Unfortunately, in most educational systems around the world there are many people who lose out on education – ironically the very people who would most benefit from education.

IDEAS FOR COMMUNICATING THE MESSAGES

Make a list of the various benefits that can come from Inclusive Education. Have the participants work in small groups to identify the benefits that can come in the short term – within one year – and those that will require a longer time. Each group can share their answers with one another but it is important that they give a reason for why they thought the benefit would come in the short or longer term.

Concluding comment

Inclusive Education is an international endeavour to which all countries are committed through their membership of the United Nations. However words alone will not make it a reality. Equally the actions of governments are not sufficient. It requires the energies and determination of local people to bring these lofty ambitions to life. Then the hope of Nelson Mandela will be realised.

> "Disabled children are equally entitled to an exciting and brilliant future."
>
> – Nelson Mandela

CHAPTER 3:
Family Involvement

This chapter examines the vital contribution that all families make to children's education. This is especially so when a child has special needs. The efforts of teachers and of parents to help the child grow and development are much more effective when they work in partnership (Mittler, 1995). More broadly, this training unit describes practical ways in which families can be supported in low-income countries. This needs to start before the child starts school. We review ways in which this could happen. The same strategies can also be used by schools to promote greater involvement of parents in their child's education.

We recognise that families can take many different forms beyond the traditional two parent family. Many children are reared by grandparents, single parents – mothers especially - as well as child-headed households. However for simplicity we use the term 'parent' to mean any of these individuals who have parenting responsibilities for the child.

The impact of poverty, poor housing and illness often compounds the difficulties these families face in bringing up a child with disabilities. Hence many families require support beyond what schools can reasonably be expected to provide. This is why inclusive education has to form part of a broad community development agenda.

Key Learning Messages

Inclusive education cannot come about without the involvement and cooperation of families. Children do their best at school when families take a close interest in their schooling. Equally parents and grandparents are likely to be the people who know the children best. Trainees need to learn that:

- The negative attitudes of parents can be changed and positive ones nurtured.
- Children learn all their basic life skills in the home and with the assistance of their parents, siblings and grandparents.
- Parents can be supported in various low-cost ways – through the provision of information, contacts with other parents, advice and guidance from early intervention.
- Children do best at school when teachers and parents work in partnership.

Rationale for family involvement

In most cultures around the world, the reactions of families to the birth of a child with a disability are similar, as are the reactions of wider society.

- The family is stigmatised when a child is born with severe disability.
- Sometimes the father is ashamed and blames the mother and leaves the family home.
- Neighbours and other children avoid visiting and fear the child.
- The child is kept indoors lying down and gradually becomes more and more dependent and with few opportunities to learn, to grow and develop.
- Families may spend a lot of money on seeking cures that do not work.
- Mothers especially become increasingly over-worked and because they do not know how to help the child; they become stressed. Their physical and mental health suffers.
- Family members may begin to neglect/ abuse the child, who may now be too heavy to lift and doubly incontinent.

The child's inclusion within society has to start with being included within the family. This then means:

- Parents are a role model for how other family members and the wider community react to the child. The child's disability is viewed more positively.

- Parents know their child's like and dislikes; their talents as well as their weaknesses. They can advise others on how best to manage the child.

- Children spend most of their time with families, even when they are attending school. The home provides plenty of opportunities to advance the child's learning.

- Families can spend more time with individual children compared to teachers or other professionals.

- Families can introduce the child to community activities and events in ways that no one else can – such as community celebrations, religious attendance, use of community facilities.

- Parents are a good source of advice for teachers and other professionals involved with the child.

Responsibilities and expectations of parenthood

We need also to recognise the important educational role that parents have in the life of all children and in some instances remind parents of their responsibilities as necessary. Parents should:

- Respect all children's rights to education, health care, love, and affectionate, inclusion, security; regardless of the disability or special needs.

- Provide for their daily needs such as food, shelter and clothes.

- Support and encourage their children's learning.

- Help them acquire basic life skills such as personal care, communication and mobility.

- Understand that some children need more time to learn than others.

- Develop sincere interest in their child's school activities.

- Observe if the children enjoy school or thrive socially.

Schools too have similar responsibilities for all their learners. Hence they are likely to provide a better education if they work in partnership with parents. The onus is on schools to ensure that personal invitations are extended to parents and they are warmly welcomed into the schools. When they were children this probably did not happen so they may not expect to be involved in their child's education or be shy to ask for this to happen. Hence, schools need to:

- Encourage attendance at Parent-teachers meetings

- Invite parents to planning meetings to discuss the child's Individual Education Programme and progress in school.

- Persuade parents to assist with the child's homework.

- Recruit parents as members of school committees

- Train parents to advocate and lobby for their rights and those of their child (see Chapter 4).

However, parents need extra support in order to play a full part in helping the child to be more included within the family from an early age. This Unit focuses on the selected themes that have been shown to be especially supportive to parents in many countries around the world. In particular, in the three countries where the inclusive education initiatives were started, parent associations were formed to support the inclusive education approach.

The main themes in this training unit

Four themes feature in this Unit.

- We examine the myths surrounding disability that can have a profound impact on families.

- We explain the success of home-based interventions for supporting families in helping their disabled child.

- We promote the formation of parent support groups locally as well as nationally.

- We describe the links that can be forged between home and school.

Theme 1: Overcoming the Myths of Disability

It has long been recognised that most parents often go through similar emotional reactions after giving birth to a child with impairments. The first is that of immediate shock:

- Every pregnant woman expects to bear a healthy, lively baby. No parent would expect a disabled baby. Parents of children with disability are psychologically, emotionally and socially unprepared. They tend to feel isolated, frustrated, disappointed, guilty and lost.

- These feelings lead some parents to reject their children with disabilities and wish that they were dead or not theirs at all. A few mothers will abandon their babies in hospital.

This stage of shock can give way to anger and blame.

- Parents, like wider society, may be ignorant about the causes of disability, such as diseases, heredity and birth traumas. They can imagine that they or their partner are to blame or they will seek to blame others.

- The presence of a disabled child may cause family disharmony such as parents blaming each other for the stigma the birth brings on the family.

- The community may believe in superstition and witchcraft, thereby causing instability and shame with neighbours.

Parents may despair and feel helpless and hopeless.

- They may be unaware that children with disabilities can still acquire normal milestones in their development and that with support they can lead a productive life.

- Most parents do not know what to do with their children with disabilities or who might be able to assist them. They need to be told about any early identification and intervention supports, medical and therapeutic services, and early childhood education and schooling.

One common way in which parents cope is to deny that there is anything wrong with the child. Parents may refuse to listen to advice, or go around different doctors or traditional healers in search of a cure. They do not want to accept that their child has a life-long impairment.

Not all disabilities are evident at birth. Some inexperienced parents may fail to detect developmental delays in their child and as a result the disability is detected very late. They may be reluctant to follow the advice of professionals, denying that there is anything wrong with their child.

What helps parents?

Parents need opportunities to share their feelings about disabilities. Opportunities to meet and talk with other parents have proved valuable in helping them to gain new perspectives. Parents can be put in touch with other parents in their neighbourhood.

Families need to be given factual information about the causes of disabilities and how the child might be helped. Seeing examples of children and adults with disabilities involved in everyday activities or gainfully employed has proved effective.

The wider family circle, especially grandparents, can exert an important influence on parents; hence opportunities should be sought to keep them informed as well.

The wider community needs to be educated about disability. The community plays a very important role in helping families adjust to having a child who is different. Many parents have found their communities can be very persecuting; they become the judges and juries and cause more pain. Local beliefs and superstitions about the causes of disability need to be named and challenged.

The prevention of further occurrences of handicapping conditions in the family is very important. Older mothers have a greater risk of having a child with intellectual impairments. Marriage between cousins has an increased risk of children being born with impairments. Young children can become disabled through illnesses such as measles, meningitis and cerebral malaria. Vaccinations are important. Pregnant women need good antenatal care. Further information is contained in the Facts for Life booklet from UNICEF (2010).

IDEAS FOR COMMUNICATING THE MESSAGES

- Parents who have a child with a disability can be invited to come and speak to the group about their feelings and experiences.
- Organise a workshop or awareness-raising event on causes of disabilities.

Theme 2: Home-based Interventions

Home-based programmes for preschoolers with disabilities have proved successful internationally (O'Toole, 1988) and have been implemented in various African countries such as Zimbabwe (Mariga and McConkey, 1987). The basic idea is simple. A person regularly visits the family at home to advise on how best to assist the child's development and to give emotional and practical support to the parents. Early identification of a child's difficulties from birth onwards with appropriate interventions from an early age can minimise the severity of the disability and this can lead to more successful school placement. These programmes often form part of Community-Based Rehabilitation services (see Chapter 6).

Home-based early intervention programmes have proved to be effective because they:

- Can reach more people than centred-based approaches.
- Equip the children, their families and community members with skills and knowledge to function better in their own communities.
- Helps the community to understand and accept the target group.
- Enable families to work with professionals and take major roles in teaching of their children.

Objectives of the home-based programme

Although the programmes can vary in the way they work with families, they often have common objectives, which are:

- To provide basic knowledge to families and community members on how to identify disabilities and design programs to promote their development.
- To teach parents ways of helping the children to acquire basic life skills.
- To encourage siblings to understand and help, thus building inclusion in the home.
- To give families have clear understanding on causes of disabilities.
- To know and understand that children with disabilities have rights.
- To promote the child's inclusion within local communities and facilities such as crèches and preschools.

Recruiting home visitors

Home visitors can be recruited from at least three different sources, and around the world, projects invariably use some combination of these. First, existing personnel are redeployed to act as home visitors. Teachers, therapists, and health workers have adopted this new style of working rather than solely seeing families in hospital clinics or disability centres. Also primary health care workers can be trained to take on this role (see chapter 6).

Second, home visitors are paid employees who have been recruited and trained specifically for this role. Although the original idea was to recruit people from the community, in later years an increasing number of people with disabilities or parents of children with disabilities have been successfully employed as home visitors. This strategy not only gives much needed employment opportunities, but these individuals come with personal insights and motivation that can make them more effective and acceptable to families.

Volunteer workers form a third option. Some community services use family members as their primary workers, whereas other community programs have successfully recruited teachers and health workers, among others, to act as voluntary supporters for families.

However, the qualities that home visitors bring to the job, rather than the background from which they come, ultimately appear to contribute more to their effectiveness. In particular, it is important that home visitors do the following:

- **Empathise with the culture of the family.** Families are then more accepting and trusting of them.

- **Respond practically to the family's needs.** Parents should experience some immediate benefits from having a home visitor.

Although the options for finding effective home visitors are available in most communities around the world, a great deal of effort needs to be expended on recruiting suitable persons because of the inevitable turnover that occurs with poorly paid or volunteer workers. Schools are well placed to help with the recruitment and training of home visiting personnel.

The training for home visiting personnel needs to prepare them to deal with a range of topics. These include:

- Skills in screening children and identifying different impairments such as hearing loss.
- Referrals to hospitals and other services.
- Listening to and counseling families and persons with disabilities.
- Challenging community attitudes to disability and myths about the causes.
- Assessing resources available in the local community.
- Beliefs about, and stages in child development.
- The management of 'problem' behaviour.
- Devising of aids and equipment (see Chapter 6 for further details).

Outcomes

International experience in Africa (Mariga and McConkey, 1987) and elsewhere confirms the following outcomes from home-based intervention:

- The family has access to aids and equipment that assist their management of the child at home.
- The children make better developmental progress.
- The parents are more confident in working with their son or daughter.
- The families have greater access to other support services.
- The parents become advocates for themselves and their children.
- The parents are more likely to seek mainstream education for their children.

IDEAS FOR COMMUNICATING THE MESSAGES

- View a video programme that shows an example of home-based intervention (see References).
- Brain-storm opportunities for starting home-based early intervention in your region or country.
- Invite a person with experience of home-based intervention as a speaker.

Theme 3: Parent Support Groups

In many countries around the world, parents benefit greatly from the support of other parents who have children with disabilities. This support has come primarily from associations formed and organised by parents. These groups may come together locally or be part of a national organisation. If none exists within a locality, schools or health personnel can encourage their formation by working alongside some interested parents.

Although varying in size and sophistication, these associations commonly fulfill three main functions: providing parents with solidarity, information and advocacy.

Solidarity: The heart-ache that comes from feeling alone with a problem can be assuaged by meeting others who have been through or who are going through similar experiences. Equally it is easier to join others to challenge prevailing attitudes and practices in society rather than to take action single-handed. Membership can also boost self-confidence and help to create a sense of pride in having a child with disability. This appears to be best fostered at a local level; hence national associations need to develop a network of branches.

Information: Parents bemoan the lack of information that is available to them even when they have access to a range of professionals. Often the need is for information that is tailored to their present needs and concerns and presented to parents in readily accessible ways. In Lesotho, southern Africa, the leaders of nine branches linked to the national parent associations identified the following needs for their parents (McConkey and Mphole, 2000):

- Knowing how to assess, teach and handle their child.
- Ways of raising parental awareness and of mobilising parents.
- Rights of people with disability.
- Disability issues generally.
- Working alongside professionals, report writing for committee members.
- Making teaching aids and equipment.

Parent associations often produce newsletters for their members; most organise meetings, conferences and training events with invited speakers; some have telephone help-lines and other employ 'parent advisers' or development workers to provide information and training for their members. You should compile a list of national associations to which you can refer parents.

Advocacy: Advocacy means speaking on behalf of, or in favour of somebody or an issue. In the three countries where Inclusive Education was initiated, the formation and strengthening of a parent organisation was a very important priority. They were supported to organise themselves to take action, such as persuading and influencing those who hold governmental positions and political powers, to adopt and implement inclusive policies. In the next chapter we will explore this function in more detail.

Being associated with a group can give parents the strength to speak up as individuals when they approach local schools to enroll their child for example - or if they have a dispute with their child's teachers. It may also give them much needed emotional support if they have problems within the family and help mothers especially to be more assertive in their dealings with in-laws or fathers.

IDEAS FOR COMMUNICATING THE MESSAGES
- Invite a representative from a local parent group or association to speak about their work.
- Have participants discuss why parents may be reluctant to join a group for parents. What might encourage them to do so?

Theme 4: Home–School Partnerships

Children do best at school when families take a close interest in their schooling. Some parents may be reluctant to contact the teachers in case they are thought to be interfering or perhaps they themselves had bad experiences at school. Teachers need to make parents feel welcomed. Because parents and grandparents are likely to be the people who know the child best, they are a good source of advice for teachers and they form the child's main educators outside of school.

Yet the inclusion of parents in the education of their children is largely hampered by the prevailing philosophy of professionalism that exists in education circles. Teachers, therapists or other professionals are regarded as the most knowledgeable people who know what is best for children with disabilities. In order to promote the involvement of parents in inclusive education perhaps there is first a need to put in place legislation that makes it a right for parents to be involved in their child's education. This has happened in countries such as the USA and the United Kingdom.

Parents and professionals should have closer collaboration with regard to inclusive education. This will enable policy makers to formulate relevant policies for their country that are based on reality rather than blurred understandings from textbooks.

Schools need to welcome parents. Here are ideas that schools around the world are using. Some parents are more willing than others to become involved. Start with the willing parents and use them to encourage others to join in (Hornby, 1995).

- Brochures about the school should be available to parents to read before the child starts school so that they understand what the school requires and how it is run.

- Parents are invited to meet the child's teacher at least once a year to discuss progress.

- Parents are involved in drawing up the individual educational plan for the child with special needs.

- Parents are invited to visit their child's class. They can see the teaching methods used in the class.

- Teachers are willing to visit the family at home. This lets them see how the child gets on there.

- Reports on the children's progress are sent to the parents every term. These reports should be detailed and clear. They might indicate areas in which work at home could complement that being done at school.

- Parents can enrich the cultural and ethnic diversity within schools by consulting with them on school practices and involving them in special events and festivals that celebrate their culture.

- Parents can help to make the school premises more accessible: for example installing ramps and improving toilet facilities.

- Parents are encouraged to assist children with their homework. They sign the child's work.

- A notebook goes between home and school with the child each day or at least every week. Teachers and parents can exchange information about the child's schoolwork and learning. Should the family not read, they should find a friend or neighbour to do the reading and writing for them.

- Parents are asked to help with activities outside school hours, such as sports, choir and school outings.

- Parents may be able to arrange work placements for senior pupils so that they acquire practical skills in realistic employment settings.

- Parents can be invited to join some of the training courses that are organised for teachers.

- Short training courses and seminars can be organised for parents. These should focus on practical activities that parents could use at home to help the child learn new skills. Teachers can arrange for visiting speakers to come to these courses.

- * Parents who have children with disabilities are assisted to form a local association. Parents can learn from one another. Visiting speakers can talk to the group and answer their questions. The group can press politicians for further help. Parents can be put in touch with the national associations for parents of disabled children. Often they have booklets they can send parents. They may have local branches that parents can join.

- Representatives from the parent groups can be invited or elected to join the Board of Management for the school.

Ideas for communicating the messages

- Divide the participants into small groups and ask them to discuss: "Why are some teachers and schools reluctant to involve parents in the life of the school?" How can they be persuaded to change their attitudes?
- Have the group brain-storm the disadvantages to the children whose parents do not communicate with the teacher. Then ask them to identify ways of improving communication.

Parent Associations in Southern Africa

Lesotho Society of Mentally Handicapped Persons (LSMHP)
P.O. Box 9204
Lesotho
Email: lsmhp@lesoff.co.za

Zanzibar Association for People with Developmental Disabilities (ZAPDD).
P.O. Box 4339
Zanzibar
Email: zapdd@znlink.com

Tanzania Association for Mentally Handicapped (TAMH)
P.O. Box 70236
Dar Es Salaam
Tanzania
Email: tamh.iep@bol.co.tz

Zimbabwe Parents of Handicapped Children Association (ZAPHCA)
P.O. Box CY 2980
Causeway
Harare
Email: zapdca@zol.co.zw

Parents of Disabled Children Association of Malawi (PODCAM)
P.O. Box 80103
Blantyre
Email: podcam@malawi.net

CHAPTER 4:
Promoting Advocacy and Empowerment

The rights of children with disabilities to inclusive education need to be fought for. Educational systems that were not designed to be inclusive will not easily give children this right. The people best placed to make the argument are those who stand most to gain from it – namely people with disabilities, or in the case of children, their parents and relatives. They need to become advocates for inclusive education. But often these are the very people who are marginalised and powerless within society. They need to become empowered in order to be effective advocates. Hence this chapter is about strengthening their voices and finding ways of ensuring they are heard.

Key Learning Messages

- All over the world, parents of children with disabilities have risen to the challenge of becoming advocates for their sons and daughters. They need support to do this: first from other parents but also from concerned professionals in their locality such as head teachers and health workers.

- People with disabilities have come together in local groups and national associations to advocate for their rights. They too can be powerful allies in promoting inclusive education.

- The voice of children and young people is often overlooked in creating better schools. We describe ways in which older pupils especially, can be empowered and encouraged to speak up for their rights.

The need for advocacy and empowerment

Empowerment can be defined as an enabling process enhancing people's capacity and will to direct and control their own lives in accordance with their needs and aspirations - as each one of us aims to direct and control our own life. One effect of empowerment is that people feel confident and able to speak out about their situation.

Advocacy is a noble pursuit. It aims to change society and its institutions by removing injustices, and creating a more equitable society. Although the voices of one or two persons can make a difference, their messages are more likely to be heard when they come together as an association. It is even better if local associations are part of a national organisation. In nearly all African countries, there are now national parent organisations and disabled person's organisation (DPOs).

Local and national organisations help to empower their members which in turns makes their advocacy more effective. Empowering parents and persons with disabilities themselves on their rights is the key to the success of any inclusion initiative. Armed with information, they can positively fight for change and challenge their national governments for inclusion. At one conference, a self-advocate stated: "We want education, employment, to be independent, to marry, acquire skills, trained in modern technology, need assistance to choose right skills, schools to be accessible and inclusive and that society must stop discriminating people with developmental disabilities".

As a result of empowerment, the same groups can monitor policies and identify gaps, and with support from professionals effect change through pressuring different sectors of the government. They can question the policy makers when policies are not implemented.

Parents and people with disabilities can also participate in decision-making and help to ensure that best practices are adopted when policies are being implemented nationally and locally.

Parent associations and DPOs can organise events to profile issues of concern and gain the interest of media such as radio and newspapers.

Belonging to an advocacy organisation has personal benefits for the members. They are empowered in knowing the causes of disabilities, what is happening in other countries and developments taking place in their own country. They can receive training in how to advocate and lobby. They can be signposted to other organisations or people who can assist them. They can become role models for other parents.

National associations may support individual members as they confront local issues, such as school enrolment or police refusing to prosecute a rapist of a lady with intellectual disabilities.

Obstacles to advocacy

Encouraging people with disabilities or parents to become active advocates is not easily achieved as they have little spare energy or motivation to embark on what can be a demanding role as an advocate for themselves and others. Other common problems also arise.

- A lack of clear vision and goal for the parent associations or the DPO. People argue about what they want the association to do.

- Lack of information and training on rights, policies, strategies to bring about change. People do not have access to people who can assist them.

- Lack of skills among the members to interpret information and foresee its consequences. In the three African countries, the parents association was also open to friends (e.g. siblings, teachers and other professionals) so that they could attract a wider membership.

- Donor dependency, lack of resources and problems with sustainability when leaders leave.

- Poor networking among parents and memberships. Low attendance at meetings. Leaders need to be committed to working as a team to share the work and get the jobs done.

- Conflicts of interests among members, sometimes hidden agendas. Members need to have trust in one another.

- Fear of intimidation or threats from those in key positions that discourage others from speaking out.

Hence parents and disabled people often need the support of like-minded peers, professionals and communities to instigate and sustain their advocacy.

Their advocacy role is likely to be more effective if alliances are made with other organisations who share a common interest; most notably among organisations of people with disabilities. In many countries there is now some form of national disability council that brings together all the disability organisations, including parents and friends associations.

The main themes in this training unit

The remainder of the chapter examines at how advocacy and empowerment can be nurtured with three groups: Parents; Disabled Persons and Disabled Youth in Schools.

Theme 1: Parent Advocacy

This theme follows on from the involvement of parents with schools that was covered in Chapter 3. Here our focus is on helping groups of parents to come together to advocate for their children's education.

In the three countries, a Norwegian NGO, known as NFU, sponsored the development of parent associations with Lilian Mariga acting as an adviser. She worked to strengthen the national associations that had started as well as fostering the development of local branches. This was achieved primarily through the provision of training workshops allied with some financial support.

Members were trained on causes of disabilities, prevention and intervention strategies, leadership, advocacy, lobbying, rights and inclusion. The associations helped to raise awareness of disability in their communities as well as nationally. They demanded their rights in national and international conferences. They have met with ministers and senior officials in government. They participated in teacher training; sharing information on how parents react to a child with special needs. They motivated other families and community members to value education. The parents worked hard to encourage parents to place their children in regular schools.

The southern region now has strong self- advocacy groups who through training became empowered and can participate and present their needs with minimum help.

IDEAS FOR COMMUNICATING THE MESSAGES

View Programme 1 on the Zanzibar Association for People with Developmental Disabilities (ZAPDD) on You Tube (see p.11) or on the DVD Inclusion in Action. The programme describes how the Association developed and the range of activities it is involved in. The programme is introduced by Lilian Mariga, NFU consultant in Eastern and Southern Africa, with the commentary provided by the Chairperson of ZAPDD, Obeid Fabian Hofi.

Local parent associations

This book can be used with existing parent associations to inform them about inclusive education. Equally it might form the basis for a group of parents to meet and study it together and out of which a local advocacy group could emerge.

Thereafter, there are a number of roles that the local parents association can play:

- Recruiting more parents to join the association or forming other groups linked to local schools.

- Organising social events to attract parents to attend meetings and to help build a sense of solidarity among members.

- Mobilising and educating other parents on policy issues and their gaps in provision in their locality.

- Engaging with people who have an interest and commitment to inclusive policies. People could be invited to attend the parent meeting and to help plan actions to be taken locally.

- Collecting information, analysing and understanding what it means in regards to inclusion. These could involve examining proposed legislations, policy statements as well as collating example of discriminatory practices.

- Building contacts in newspapers and local radio who will communicate your message.

- Linking with other parent associations to assist with exchange of information and provide mutual support to one another.

- Identify the role of community and national leaders in effecting laws and policies. Seek meetings with them to explain what needs to change.

- Participating in awareness raising events within community and contributing to training courses; e.g. in-service training courses for teachers or health workers (McConkey et al., 2000).

Tips for success

Advocacy is not an easy road to travel. Being prepared for possible difficulties is a step to their solution. Here are some lessons we have learnt.

- Deal with conflicts within the group. Better to bring issues out into the open so that they can be discussed and a compromise reached.

- The strength and impact of advocating comes from doing the work not from members adopting a 'wait-and-see' attitude or being content to sit on the sidelines.

- Associations should always document their processes so that newcomers understand the work that has been carried out.

- Advocacy needs to focus on the source of problem for it to be effective. Beware of getting distracted on what could be minor issues rather than dealing with bigger issues.

- Make clear the messages you want to communicate to others. Prepare your arguments well and practice beforehand if you are speaking at meetings. Also it is good to anticipate the questions you might be asked and to have answers ready.

- Don't try to do too much too quickly. It is better to prioritise the key issues and put your energies into making a difference. Also don't be too ambitious: as they say, you have to crawl before you can walk. Early successes will help build confidence and skills.

- It is easy to get downhearted when disappointments come but try to maintain positive beliefs and attitudes. Remind yourself of your successes – celebrate them!

> **IDEAS FOR COMMUNICATING THE MESSAGES**
>
> - Contact the national parent association to learn about their programme of activities and how they might be able to assist local schools.
> - Meet with a group of parents to discuss the idea of starting a parent association. Identify the benefits they see to having an association, the barriers they might face to belonging to such an association and the supports they would like the organisation to provide to members.

Theme 2: Disabled People's Organisations (DPOs)

In most countries of the world, there are national organisations of disabled people usually for different impairment groups, such as blind, deaf and physically impaired. In the past these were often charitable agencies set up by able-bodied persons to provide help for people with these particular impairments. Internationally there has been a shift from organisations that do things for people with disabilities towards those made up of persons with disabilities who speak and do things for themselves. In fact, the slogan that originated in South Africa, "Nothing about us without us" is a clear reflection of the movement towards self-determination and self-representation of people with disabilities.

However, both types of organisations may still co-exist within countries and they too can prove useful allies for schools. In some countries there may be local branches as well as national head-quarters that you can contact. Also DPOs in other countries often have web-sites that contain a wealth of information about disabling conditions.

Disabled people have articulated their support for Inclusive Education through their organisations in southern Africa which together form a federation known as the Southern Africa Federation of Organisations of Disabled people (SAFOD). They argue strongly against a segregated approach to the education of disabled children. They see access to education as a basic right for all disabled children which should be realised through the strategy of equalisation of opportunities. They endorse Article 24 of the UN Convention (see following page).

Enlisting the help of DPOs

The national association may be able to put you in contact with local branches. If none exist you might call a meeting of disabled persons in your locality. You should be able to identify them through your personal contacts or via community leaders and health personnel. Here are some ways in which local and national DPOs can assist schools, students and families.

- They can provide more information about the causes of particular disabilities and how they can be overcome. Most have information leaflets and booklets available free of charge.
- They can give information about the availability of aids and appliances that can make life easier for children with disabilities and their families.
- They may be able to advise parents on the services and financial benefits to which they are entitled and help them gain access to them.
- They can act as advocates for individual children in accessing services and supports and also assist with advocating for greater access to education and employment.
- They can be invited to contribute to training courses for parents, teachers and the wider community; for example, teaching sign language.
- They may be able to identify mentors for learners with particular disabilities who can advise and counsel them when they face particular challenges or choices.

> "States Parties shall ensure an inclusive education system at all levels and life long learning …. In realizing this right, States Parties shall ensure that … Persons with disabilities are not excluded from the general education system on the basis of disability, and that children with disabilities are not excluded from free and compulsory primary education, or from secondary education, on the basis of disability".
>
> – Article 24: Education from UN Convention on the Rights of Persons with Disabilities

A caution

One word of caution: some DPOs may favour special schooling and are sceptical of inclusive schools. Their viewpoint needs to be heard and respected. Perhaps it is not a case of arguing which option is best but rather of thinking how the particular needs of children with severe hearing or visual problems can be met in a locality. A step wise approach to inclusion could be negotiated. In the three African countries, special units were first established within an ordinary school for a group of such children with particular disabilities e.g. children with blindness and deafness. These classes were taught by a specialist trained teacher. However the children were encouraged to join the regular classes for non-academic subjects and to mix at free times.

As the teachers became more confident and received training, the students in these specialised classes were assessed for progress and transferred to regular classes for some of the subjects on the curriculum. This second step provided a bridge between the special unit and the mainstream classes. The third step is for children to receive all their education within mainstream classes and for the specialist teacher to act as a mentor and guide for other teachers in the school; supplemented with some individual teaching of pupils according to their needs.

Partnerships with DPOs

The relationships between schools and DPOs can be taken further as these examples from Zanzibar demonstrate. We suspect that DPOs will be willing partners in helping schools to ensure there is education for all children.

- DPOs were invited to nominate representatives to the national steering committee for the Inclusive Education Programme. Their insights and aspirations helped to shape the programme nationally and their advocacy was important to maintain its work.

- At a local level, members of DPOs joined the Inclusive Education Committees within schools and took part in training courses for teachers.

- In one school, a father with disabilities became chairperson of the Parents Association (see photo). This provided a very strong message about the school's commitment to inclusion.

IDEAS FOR COMMUNICATING THE MESSAGES

- Identify the Disabled People's Organisations in your country – the telephone directory or internet search is a good starting point. There may also be an umbrella organisation for all DPOs – get a list of their members. Ask for volunteers to make contact with each of the DPOs identified to find out what information and services they have available. Collect this information so that it can be shared.

- Invite a representative from a DPO to visit the school and talk about their work and views on inclusive education.

Theme 3: Advocacy and Disabled Youth

In Zanzibar donor funding from Norway also included a Youth Development Programme aimed at youth with disabilities who had dropped out of secondary schools. A fulltime co-ordinator was appointed and he used the parent association local branch network to recruit members. A range of educational opportunities was developed around teenage issues such as HIV and AIDS as well as undertaking work experience with local businesses and participating in team sports, such as basketball. Able-bodied students were easily recruited to play alongside their peers with disabilities on the same team and to take part in after-school training and informal competitions.

However the skills and confidence of the young people to become advocates also developed. This was evident in their interactions with non-disabled youth in the team sports, the impact they had on spectators who watched them playing and also on the fellow workers when they undertook work placements. Their families felt they had improved and were proud of their achievements.

The young people went on to devise role plays and dramas about reactions to disability and they performed these for school children in local schools (see Photo). These were especially well received by pupils, not least because they featured local people of their age.

All this work is not just for the present but it helps to prepare young people with disabilities to become active citizens in their community once they leave school. From among them, the future leaders of DPOs will emerge.

Hence schools need to think about how they can nurture the advocacy of all their pupils but especially those with special needs.

IDEAS FOR COMMUNICATING THE MESSAGES

View Programme 6 on Skills Training for Youth in YouTube (see page 11) or in the DVD Inclusion in Action. This video programme describes the work undertaken within schools and outside of schools which was described above. The commentary is provided by Mr Juma Salim, coordinator of the Youth Development Programme in Unguja, Zanzibar.

Promoting pupil advocacy

Here are some of the ways schools promoted pupil advocacy for inclusive education:

- Student representatives were included on the Inclusive Education Committees set up by the schools. They took part in the meetings alongside parents, teachers and community representatives.

- Students with disabilities would be involved alongside other members of Inclusive Education Committee when they were meeting local officials or politicians.

- Youth with disabilities were included as members of the student councils for the schools.

- Pupils elected their head boy and head girl. Pupils were nominated and elections were held. In one school, a young man with intellectual disabilities was elected as Head Boy.

- Students with disabilities were given particular responsibilities within the school. This brought them into contact with teachers and pupils and demonstrated their abilities.

- An art competition was held to design a poster promoting inclusive education. The winners were displayed at a special exhibition.

- Disabled pupils were encouraged to participate in all school activities – sports teams, choir, dance groups – according to their talents and interests.

Some of the problems that can arise are similar to those noted earlier for parents. But perhaps the biggest problem is that we don't believe that the young people with disabilities will be able to advocate for themselves and so we do not even give them the opportunity to learn (Lewis, 2007).

> IDEAS FOR COMMUNICATING THE MESSAGES
> - List the ways in your school currently encourages the advocacy of pupils. Are any pupils with disabilities involved in these activities?
> - Debate the benefits and disadvantages of starting a club for disabled teenagers that would meet after school.

Concluding comment

The chapter takes seriously the slogan of the disabled people's movement internationally: Nothing about us without us! Educationalists who wish to promote inclusive education must ensure that people with disabilities and their parents are actively engaged in the endeavour and not left as mere spectators. This requires extra efforts but it ensures that inclusive education will be better suited to the needs of the local people with a greater chance of sustainability in the longer term.

CHAPTER 5:
Involving Local Communities

Schools thrive best when they are fully part of their local community. This is especially true for schools that aspire to be fully inclusive. So we want to break down the glass wall that surrounds too many schools because they keep students in and the community out! In this chapter we examine what it means for schools to become more involved with their local community. In order for inclusive education to be really successful, schools need to make links with the different people and groups that are found in most communities, as the above diagram shows. By enlisting their help, schools will provide a richer education for all students as well as those with special needs; supporting the truth of the proverb.

> It takes a village to educate a child
>
> – African proverb

Key Learning Messages

All schools are already part of a community. The children live locally as do most teachers. Along with the children's parents they already have personal connections to many different people in the local community. Through these personal connections, local people can become more involved with the school and its inclusive activities. But this requires active planning by schools.

- People in the community can hold negative attitudes to children with disabilities. But these attitudes can be changed.

- Schools need to educate the local communities about their ambitions and seek their assistance in making them a reality.

- People from the community can be invited to join the committee that is guiding the development of inclusive education within the school.

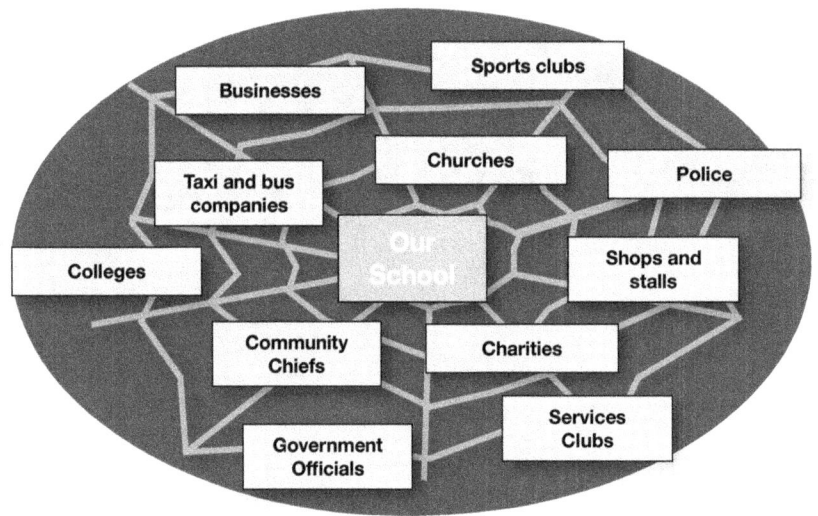

Rationale for Community Involvement

In affluent countries of Europe and the Americas with an abundance of financial capital, there is growing appreciation that wealth alone is not sufficient for building strong communities. Politicians such as Bill Clinton in the USA and Tony Blair in the UK, often spoke of the need to rebuild what has been termed 'social capital'. This refers to the social bonds that underpin the functioning of communities and the civic endeavours of its citizens that contribute to the common good. Without this form of social capital, people's lives will be poorer.

This analysis has powerful messages for people with disabilities. They are among the most marginalised in our society (Emerson et al. 2008). They lack the financial capital to make life better and have little political capital to influence society. It is especially crucial then that they can access the social capital within their communities if they are to enjoy a better life.

As noted in Chapter 1, it has been proposed that social capital is made up of three components – bonding, bridging and linking. These capture well the rationale and strategies required to build support for inclusive education within communities. Table 5.1 gives some specific examples of how social capital was nurtured within the three African countries. Later in this chapter we will give further examples of how links can be made with community leaders, politicians and government officials; how bridging social capital can be created within local communities and how school communities can become better bonded.

TABLE 5.1: EXAMPLES OF BUILDING SOCIAL CAPITAL	
Bonding	Teachers and parents gathered at the school to plan strategies for greater community participation. People from the community were invited to join the Inclusive Education Committee within the school.
Bridging	Bridges were built between the schools and the local health services so that students with special needs could be assessed for hearing and vision problems. A local business man provided a school with a vacant shop to sell goods so that funds could be raised for the Inclusive Education programme.
Linking	In Zanzibar links were formed between schools and the village chiefs who provide local government in the islands. They in turn made contact with politicians and senior officials in government departments. In Lesotho linkages were made with the local newspapers and radio stations who carried success stories around children's inclusion as a way of educating the community about disability.

In other chapters we will also show how social capital can also be built with health services (Chapter 6) and within educational systems (Chapters 7 onwards).

> IDEAS FOR COMMUNICATING THE MESSAGES
>
> - Look again at the diagram at the start of this section and make a similar diagram of the different groups in your local community who could be of assistance to schools. This is sometimes called 'community mapping' or making an appraisal of community resources.
>
> - At a meeting of parents or teachers, identify those who also belong to the groups listed – perhaps a parent is a taxi driver or a teacher is married to a policeman. This will help to identify existing bonds and bridges within the community.

Changing Community Perceptions of Disability

In all cultures around the world people in local communities may hold negative attitudes towards disability. Disabled children are seen as worthless; they are a danger to others; they are a curse and bring bad luck; they are a punishment for past sins. Their impairments can be seen as infectious so neighbours instruct their children not to eat or drink food that was touched by a disabled child. Mothers of able-bodied children may forbid their child to play with the disabled child in case they get infected. Consequently parents don't want disabled children to attend the same schools as their sons and daughters. Indeed, teachers may hold similar beliefs (McConkey et al., 1999).

In recent years many of these old notions about disability have given way to more enlightened attitudes internationally. But myths can still linger on in many communities and when they are present, disabled children and their families are discriminated against – shut out of community life. The solution is obvious. Communities need to be educated about disability. People need to discover that their fears and suspicions are wrong. This has to happen locally if real change is to happen in your community. This means that local people need to become educators about disability: you cannot wait for this to happen nationally. The good news is that there are plenty of people to do this, once they are mobilised. In our experience the best educators have been:

- **Parents and older siblings of children with disabilities.** They know well the people in their community and have firsthand experience of the hurtful ways in which they have been treated.

- **People with disabilities.** Disabled adults in local communities – including older teenagers – could also be powerful change agents for the same reasons as given above for parents.

- **Head teachers and teachers.** They are well respected by local people and they have the authority and knowledge to counteract the myths that people may hold about disability.

- Health personnel. They also hold positions of trust and respect within communities. They can explain the causes of disability.

- **Religious leaders.** They have a particular role to play in contradicting some of the myths surrounding the causes of disability and also in mobilizing emotional and practical support for families.

Ideally these different groups could come together to form a partnership for educating local communities and share the work that is involved. Equally any one group can make a start.

Educating communities

Based on experience in Africa as well as internationally, four factors have proved successful in changing perceptions of disability.

Target groups. You need to focus your efforts on particular groups within your community whose attitudes you feel need to change. This will enable you to devise educational approaches that are suited to your chosen groups. For example how you educate parents should be different to what you would do with school pupils.

Planned personal contacts with disabled persons. Attitudes change when people have the opportunity to meet, talk and listen to people who are disabled. This gives people an opportunity to overcome their fears as they discover that the people they thought were very different are in fact just like themselves!

Interesting and relevant information. The emphasis needs to be on people rather than the features of their impairments. The personal attributes of individuals should be highlighted – their talents, interests and abilities. The core message is that disability does not mean inability.

Multi-media presentations. There are lots of ways of getting the message across – video, leaflets, posters, singing, drama. These will often have more impact than a person standing before a group and giving a talk! Any teacher will tell you that when learners are engaged and entertained they are more willing to be educated!

In the remainder of this chapter we will give you four examples as to how these principles were put into practice in rural African villages and townships – with community leaders; in gatherings of local communities; with school communities and with politicians and government officials. These were done at very little cost but they did require lots of energy and enthusiasm from local people to make them happen.

Remember too that community education can occur in small ways for tiny numbers of people, as well as in large scale activities aimed at big groups of people.

> **IDEAS FOR COMMUNICATING THE MESSAGES**
> - Have people list the negative attitudes society can hold about disabilities.
> - Invite people to think about what changed their attitudes to people with disabilities. What does this tell us about how we should educate communities?

Examples of Community Education

These four examples illustrate how different forms of social capital can be built – linking, bridging and bonding. They are intended as ideas to be considered and tried. They need to be adapted for each community and target groups within it.

1. Community leaders

Community leaders are very important to the implementation of inclusive education as they provide linking social capital. Here we include local chiefs, traditional healers, elected politicians and religious leaders – in short people of influence. It is courteous to inform local chiefs about your plans but this is also a good opportunity to enlist their active co-operation.

In Zanzibar, the community leaders were invited to join the Inclusive Education Committee that had been set up by the local school. (This consisted of parents of disabled students and non-disabled students, the Head Teacher and a teacher, one or more non-disabled students.) The community leaders played a key role in linking the school to community resources that they were able to mobilise alongside those recruited by parents and teachers. Here are examples of how local people assisted schools.

- Volunteers – mostly men – were sought to build or refurbish classrooms in participating schools.
- The school grounds and toilets were made more accessible for wheelchair users by building ramps (see photo on previous page).
- The community also made sure the roads or paths to the school were safe.
- Safe water points were installed at the school and in the community.

- Local communities were also encouraged to donate goods or money to help schools to purchase materials.
- Work experience and employment opportunities were sought for some young people with disabilities prior to and on leaving school.

The schools and the Inclusive Education Committees were encouraged to keep the local chiefs – Shehas – informed about the programme and to seek their assistance on making representations to Government. The local chiefs were also a conduit of information from Government and other interests in the locality. The chiefs were invited to committee meetings or else a sub-group from the committee would seek a meeting with the chief. The building of personal relationships with community leaders was seen as critical to shaping community attitudes to disabled persons. One assistant chief said this:

> "I want to get a good life for everyone in my village. Disability can come to anyone. We must communicate with these people and learn with them so that they can get jobs and some may go to university level."

2. Community gatherings

In all three countries, public meetings were held to make local people more aware of children with disabilities and to foster bridging social capital. In Lesotho for example, the national Parent Association helped local branches to organise a community gathering aimed at changing negative attitudes towards people with different abilities through creating awareness and understanding of their needs.

- Invitations were sent to key people in the community: district administrators, councillors, district education officers, chiefs and headmen, representatives of NGOs and DPOs, parents and other community members.
- The gathering was held on a Saturday afternoon when people had free time and in a public place. Posters advertising the event were placed around the area and it was publicised on local radio.
- Different groupings of parents who had a disabled child, disabled youth and teachers were organised to make presentations. These included songs, drama and role plays depicting negative attitudes but also stressing the benefits of positive attitudes towards people who are different.
- Local musicians and dancers were recruited to provide entertainment and encourage people to attend.
- The community leaders and local politicians made short speeches welcoming the new opportunities that were to be provided in the community for people with disabilities and how local people could help.

- Although designed to educate the community, this type of event had the added benefit of helping parents and disabled youth feel better about themselves - they were the centre of attention and in a sense could feel proud of their achievements.

3. Educating school communities

The same approaches can be used to help bond school communities – pupils, their parents and teachers – and make them more aware of disability and challenge negative attitudes. Here are some other ideas that were tried.

- Disabled youth in Zanzibar developed a drama about a youth who was refused entry to secondary school but showed how he was helped to challenge this decision. They visited local schools and after the drama, led a discussion with pupils and teachers about changing negative attitudes.

- A design competition was held for schools to devise a poster that showed inclusive education in action. The best posters were then painted on the school walls as a message for the wider community.

- A puppet show was used with younger children to tell the story of how a child with a disability got included in the many activities that other children did and was no longer left out.

- All the children in the class were taught basic signs so that they could communicate with a child who had hearing impairments. They also learnt a song using signs which they performed at a school concert.

- Able-bodied pupils were matched with pupils with disability from their neighbourhood whom they could accompany to/from school. This also led to some friendships being developed.

- In team sports, pupils with disabilities were recruited to play alongside their non-disabled peers on the same basketball or football team and to take part in after-school training and informal competitions. This helped to further integrate the young people with disabilities into their community beyond the school.

4. Educating politicians and government officials

Enlightened politicians like Mandela have long recognised the importance of education to nation building.

> "Education is the great engine of personal development. It is through education that the daughter of a peasant can become a doctor, that the son of a mineworker can become the head of the mine, that a child of farm workers can become the president of a great nation. It is what we make out of what we have, not what we are given, that separates one person from another."
>
> – Nelson Mandela

Yet parents and people with disabilities have a key role to play in lobbying their government for inclusive policies. This is another form of community education albeit at a national rather than local level. The parent associations in Tanzania and Zanzibar were instrumental in getting an inclusive education policy for their country. Here are some of the strategies that were used to do this.

- A politician with an interest in disability was identified. Either they had a disability or had a relative who was disabled. They became a useful allay and adviser.

- A paper was prepared that outlined the main policy actions that were required and why. This was sent to relevant officials as well as Government ministers. This outlined the United Nations Conventions and drew attention to the national constitution and the rights contained in it.

- A meeting was sought with the Minister and officials to discuss the paper. The delegation to meet the Minister was carefully chosen and each person was given a specific topic to cover. Examples of good practice in inclusive education were identified in local schools.

- The media were informed about the meeting and its outcomes.

- The minister was invited to visit schools that had implemented inclusive policies. Again this was used to get further media publicity.

- These strategies were repeated with local members of parliament. Meetings were sought with them and they were invited to visit schools. Their support was sought for the Minister to formulate and implement an inclusive education policy.

> IDEAS FOR COMMUNICATING THE MESSAGES
> - Using these examples, identify other groups in the community and brainstorm ways in which they could be better educated about people with disabilities: e.g. taxi drivers, police, shop-keepers.
> - Invite community leaders to the school to discuss your needs and how the community might assist in meeting these needs.

Concluding comment

It would easy for schools to say that working with communities is not their responsibility – their job is to teach the learners. But this argument does not recognise the outcomes that education is striving to achieve for all the learners and especially those with special needs. These could be summarised thus:

- National coverage of education.
- Equality of opportunity for all citizens.
- Respect for diversity.
- Creating empowered citizens who can contribute to society.
- Producing effective schools.

Thus inclusion is not just to give particular children a better education. Rather it recognises that education is a force for social change and for creating a more equitable society in which people with disabilities can become full and active members. This has to happen locally as well as nationally. That is the reason for the importance we place on schools actively being involved in, and working with their local communities.

CHAPTER 6:
Engaging with Community Health Services

Children with disabilities have additional health needs. This chapter focuses on how schools can work in partnerships with local health services to ensure that impairments are detected, appropriate treatments are provided, and suitable aids and appliances are supplied.

These partnerships will benefit all pupils in the school and not just those with obvious impairments. Many more children will have mild impairments that remain undetected or untreated illnesses that will interfere with their learning. The sooner these are identified and treated the better.

Schools are also an ideal location in which to base health promotion activities – for parents as well as children. This includes healthy diets, infection control and vaccinations.

Children with physical and sensory impairments will benefit from different forms of therapy. However the availability of trained therapists is limited so their time is better spent advising parents and teachers on how to carry out the necessary specialist treatments.

Key Learning Messages

- Children should be assessed to identify any impairment which parents or teachers suspect they may have.
- Schools and families need to be involved in the treatments and therapies that will reduce the child's impairments.
- Health services and schools both gain when they work closely together.

The rationale for promoting better health

It has been estimated that 65% of the disabilities affecting children are preventable. The World Health Organisation (WHO) reported in a 29-country study in Africa that the foremost cause of disability was infectious diseases such as malaria, polio, leprosy and other non-communicable diseases such as TB, trachoma, otitis media, meningitis and parasitic diseases. Other causes of disability include malnutrition due to vitamin A, iron and iodine deficiency, and chronic medical conditions such as rheumatic diseases and diabetes. Parents need to know how to prevent diseases from occurring and the importance of having children vaccinated.

The next most common cause of disability was war, trauma and accidents. The number of trauma victims who become significantly disabled following injury is reported to be far higher in Africa owing to the health care system failures. These include a lack of equipment and medical supplies at critical moments such as during pregnancy and child birth. The poor quality of peri-natal care results in disabilities such as cerebral palsy. Also the inability to afford training and hiring of specialist health care professionals contributes to higher disability prevalence rates.

The HIV and AIDS epidemic has further contributed to the prevalence of disability because many people living with HIV develop different types of impairments and functional limitations. HIV-positive infants experience an increased prevalence of cognitive and motor delay (see UNICEF, 2006 publication for details).

The third main cause of disability are congenital disabilities such as Down Syndrome. In recent years it has been shown that much can be done to enhance the development of babies born with congenital impairments through the provision of early intervention, good family support and educational opportunities.

The relationship between poverty and disability has been long established. Deprivation of basic needs – shelter, clean water, food and safety - can cause developmental delay and physical, psychological or intellectual impairment in what would be otherwise healthy children. But poverty increases the risk of infections and diseases in mothers and babies so that the children are born with impairments or soon acquire them.

The UNICEF publication – Facts for Life – gives further details. Also the World Report on Disability published by WHO-World Bank in 2011 has a chapter on Health.

The main themes in this training unit

This Unit is in three parts. The first deals with primary health workers who are present in every community around the world. The second explores links with disability specialists such as therapists. The third focuses on Community-Based Rehabilitation services which although not present in all communities, is the approach recommended by the World Health Organisation to provide assistance to persons with disabilities. There are many similarities between the philosophy and practice of Inclusive Education and CBR.

Theme 1: Partnerships with Primary Health Care Workers

In every nation of the world, families receive their primary health care from some form of community-based health workers. Although their role varies from country-to-country the core tasks usually involve health and nutrition education, instigating community activities to improve hygiene and sanitation and making referrals to higher level services such as hospital-based clinics for assessments and treatments. Family planning, prenatal care, monitoring children's growth and encouraging the uptake of vaccinations also feature in many programmes.

Schools should develop links with the primary health care staff working in their locality. Here are some of the ways they can assist children and families.

- Screening the children for possible health conditions such as chest, eye and ear infections.

- Encouraging families to provide a healthy diet and provision of clean water.

- Referring the children at early stage for medical help if they develop illnesses that may be more severe on the children because of their disabilities. See UNICEF publication on management of sick children by community health workers.

- Health workers can put families in touch with other families in the locality who may have a son or daughter similar to theirs and encourage the growth of family 'self-help' groups.

- They can support the child's engagement in community life such as their enrolment in schools, attendance at religious ceremonies through their networks and status within the community.

With additional training and appropriate support, such workers could also undertake a number of other key functions that will assist the children before they come to school as well as when they are enrolled. Experienced teachers and disability specialists could contribute to such training courses. Two areas might be worth focusing on.

- Screening children for possible sensorial and physical disabilities from 12 months onwards. For example, the high incidence of hearing problems in people with Down syndrome can easily go unrecognised and thus their ability to communicate verbally will be severely impeded. Those children who test positively will need to be referred onwards although simple guidance can be given to the health workers to impart to families when an impairment is suspected.

- Advising families on activities and routines which promote the child's physical, social and intellectual development in the pre-school years especially. Health workers might act as home visitors (see chapter 3) to advise families on play activities they can use to help the child's social and cognitive development as well as giving them suggestions to help children acquire daily living skills such as self-feeding and toileting.

However, these high ambitions for the contributions made by primary care workers can be easily frustrated unless particular care is taken on the following points:

- **Selection of Community Health workers:** The motivation and performance of workers is increased if trainees are chosen by their fellow-villagers, and after training they live and work among their own people.

- **Identification of key functions:** The effectiveness of community health workers is impaired if they are expected to undertake too many diverse tasks. This risk is high as the needs of people with disabilities vary so much according to their impairments.

- **Ongoing support and supervision is provided:** The network of local workers must be supported by personnel who have training and expertise in coping with disabilities. Extra resources are therefore needed to provide such back-up; a point we will come back to in the next section.

IDEAS FOR COMMUNICATING THE MESSAGES

- Identify the primary health workers working in your locality.
- Meet with them to find out the work they do and the contacts they have with families whose children have a disability.
- Explore the training and support they would like to have.

Theme 2: Partnerships with Health Service Personnel and Disability Specialists

In more affluent countries there are many different specialists who can assist children with disabilities. This includes doctors, psychologists, social workers, nurses and various therapists such as Physical Therapists, Occupational Therapists and Speech and Language Therapists along with more specialist staff such as audiologists (who test hearing). They are much less plentiful in many developing countries. Instead there may be more generic rehabilitation workers who have received basic training across different disciplines or who act as therapy aides in one discipline.

All of these personnel can also be a particular support to schools if they are available in the locality. Some examples are noted below but the list can be extended depending on their availability and expertise.

- Educating the community on the causes and prevention of disabilities.

- Early detection of disabilities and devising early intervention programmes for families to follow.

- Formulating stimulation programmes for child with particular impairments and working with parents and preschool educators on their implementation.

- Participating in teacher training courses; for example training them in screening tests for impairments and giving advice on managing particular disabilities within the classroom and school.

- Contributing to drawing up Individual Education plans that address the child's particular disabilities.

- Advising families and teachers on the aids and appliances that can be used to overcome the child's difficulties, for example in mobility or the vision aids that are available.

- Where appliances are used, they can advise on the position of the learner and how the aids are best maintained.

In Zanzibar for example, the national steering committee for the Inclusion Programme linked the participating schools with local health personnel who could assist them in identifying and responding to the children's individual needs. They negotiated with the Ministry of Health for their staff who worked in the locality of the participating school, to be released for short periods to assist with the assessment of children whom teachers had identified as having special needs. This included physiotherapists, occupational therapists and audiologists. A multi-disciplinary team of personnel then visited the school for half-a-day and undertook assessments as needed, of pupils' vision, hearing, motor development and fine-motor co-ordination. If possible a community mental health nurse and social worker also were present to discuss issues of concern to the family. A report was compiled on each child to be shared with parents and teachers with suggestions for classroom and teaching adaptations to suit the child's needs. Onward referrals for further examination or health treatments were made if required.

How schools could link with health personnel

- Schools should keep a list of health personnel and where they can be contacted. This list should be given to all teachers.

- Schools can offer their premises to these workers for 'clinics'; for example, to carry out health checks on children in the pre-school years. In this way, parents and pre-school children become familiar with the school.

- If teachers suspect children of having a health problem, they should refer them to these clinics.

- Health personnel can be invited to speak at parent meetings or on training courses for parents or teachers. Likewise, teachers may get invited to training courses organised for health personnel.

- Health personnel already involved with the child and family, such as therapists, can be invited to the school. They can contribute to a shared Individual Educational Plan for the child.

- Often appropriate personnel are not available. The School Board of Management should write to the health authorities and local politicians to point this out.

- Retired health workers may be willing to offer their services to the school on a voluntary basis. They could assist with developmental checks and screening for disabilities.

David Werner's manual: Disabled Village Children is a mine of information on how children with disabilities can be assisted using low-cost aids. This is available as a free download on the Internet.

> #### Ideas for communicating the messages
> - Identify the health personnel working in your locality.
> - Meet with them to discuss how schools could work more closely with them on issues such as referrals, assessments and programme planning.
> - Discuss with them, how they might provide training sessions for teachers and parents on topics that are relevant, for example making simple aids and equipment.

Theme 3: Partnerships with Community-Based Rehabilitation (CBR)

CBR activities started in the early 1980s. It has evolved from technical input for rehabilitation into the development of disabled people's capacity to advocate for their own rights along with equity of access to education and basic services. CBR aims to interlink their rehabilitation with multi-sectoral development programmes while also challenging prejudice and barriers in the community.

The CBR Matrix produced by WHO (2010) summarises the five main inter-linked strands of activities in which CBR programmes should endeavour to operate (see Figure). Education forms a major domain of activity. Through their involvement with CBR programmes, schools can also become linked with the other sectors shown in the figure as well as health.

GOAL: INCLUSIVE DEVELOPMENT ~ INCLUSIVE SOCIETY

HEALTH	EDUCATION	LIVELIHOOD	SOCIAL	EMPOWERMENT
PROMOTION	EARLY CHILDHOOD/ PRE-SCHOOL	SKILLS DEVELOPMENT	PERSONAL ASSISTANCE	SOCIAL MOBILISATION
PREVENTION	BASIC PRIMARY	SELF-EMPLOYMENT	RELATIONSHIP MARRIAGE AND FAMILY	POLITICAL PARTICIPATION
MEDICAL CARE	SECONDARY AND HIGHER	WAGE EMPLOYMENT	CULTURE RELIGION AND ARTS	COMMUNICATION
REHABILITATION	NON-FORMAL	FINANCIAL SERVICES	LEISURE RECREATION AND SPORTS	SELF-HELP GROUPS
ASSISTIVE DEVICES	LIFE-LONG LEARNING	SOCIAL PROTECTION	ACCESS TO JUSTICE	DISABLED PEOPLE'S ORGANISATIONS

The main strengths of CBR compared to tradition health services are:

– The focus is on the individual within the family and community context rather than as a patient who receives treatment.

– The programmes allow people with disabilities to participate in planning services that will directly benefit them; recipients are empowered to take responsibility for their own lives.

– CBR uses existing resources and does not require special buildings for its work. Hence it is more cost-effective.

- It draws upon local expertise and traditional wisdom in helping people with disabilities.
- CBR challenges negative attitudes and barriers in society.
- It ensures that the needs of people with disabilities are considered in community development initiatives. CBR works to promote the overall development of the community.

Schools and CBR

Here's how schools can benefit from Community-Based Rehabilitation programmes in their locality.

- CBR plays a major role in the early Identification of childhood impairments and the provision of early intervention to families.
- Education of families, teachers and the local community on the causes and types of disabilities.
- Advising families and making referrals to appropriate services.
- CBR helps parents to develop mutual support, seek schooling for their children and work cooperatively with educators.
- Linking the school to other service providers such as health, social, and community services.
- Linking the schools with families and local community leaders.
- Promoting a positive attitude to disability among families, community, schools and other service providers.
- Working with teachers and advise them on making classrooms and toilets more accessible.
- The can advise on and obtain adaptive appliances to be used in schools: e.g. walking aids to help children to be mobile, magnifiers for children with visual problems and writing aids for children with poor fine motor control.
- They can advise on how best to position children within classrooms.
- CBR staff will help devise therapy programmes to be run by families and schools to help the children overcome specific difficulties they may have in mobility or communication.

- Community-Based Rehabilitation programmes can educate families on preventable disabilities. Also educating them on how their children are vulnerable to abuse and preventing them from becoming infected with HIV.
- CBR staff can co-ordinate the contributions of different sectors to produce more effective supports for children and families.

Community-Based Rehabilitation makes sure the community is involved in giving support to their fellow citizens and increased sustainability of any educational programme.

IDEAS FOR COMMUNICATING THE MESSAGES

- Find out if there is a CBR programme working in your locality.
- Meet with them to discuss how schools could work more closely with them on issues such as referrals, assessments and programme planning.
- Discuss with them how they might provide training sessions for teachers and parents on topics that are relevant, for example, promoting advocacy and changing negative attitudes.

Concluding comment

We realise that in some localities health services are not well developed. If that is the case, then schools have an important role in advocating for better provision that will assist all their pupils as well as those with disabilities.

Schools can also make an important contribution to improving the health of the whole community by being part of campaigns for safe water, better sanitation, and the prevention of accidents and injuries such as paraffin fires.

IDEAS FOR COMMUNICATING THE MESSAGES

Programme 3: Working in Partnership in the DVD *Inclusion in Action* (downloadable through YouTube – see p.11) introduces the various partners and outlines the different contributions they made to Inclusive Education in Zanzibar. This illustrates many of the points made in this chapter.

Thanks

We are grateful to Vyvienne M"kumbuzi, Department of Physiotherapy, University of Malawi for her assistance with this chapter.

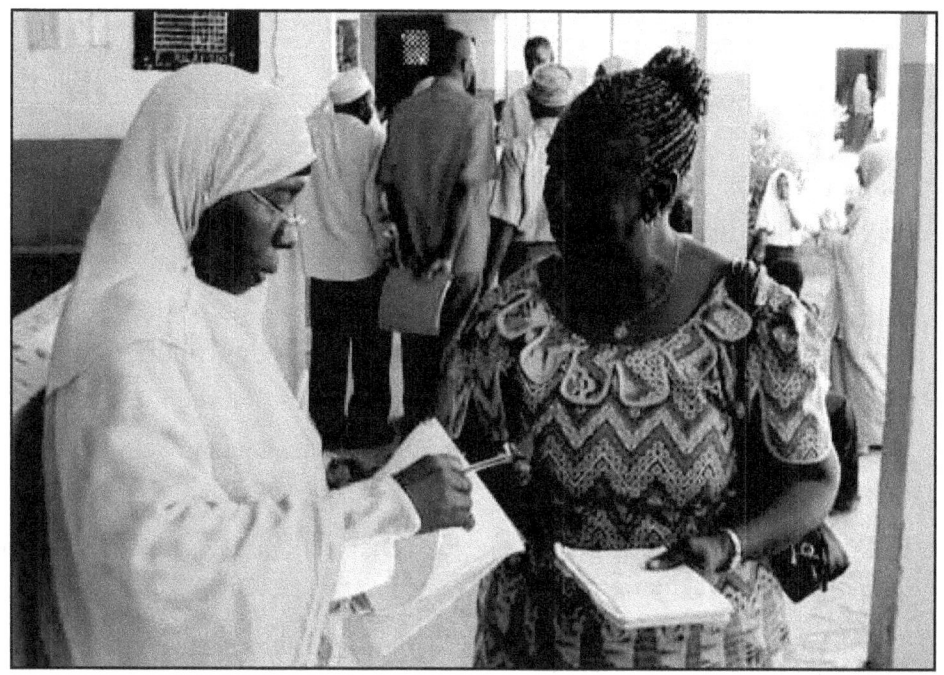

CHAPTER 7:
Conducting a Feasibility Study for Inclusive Education

In this and the following chapters, we will describe how an inclusive education policy for schools can be developed and implemented nationally. These strategies were successfully used in Lesotho from 1990 onwards and in Zanzibar and Tanzania from 2004 onwards.

We start by recapping the support arrangements that are required which we described in Chapter 1. We then describe two types of information that can be obtained from a feasibility study. Firstly, it identifies the community resources that may be available to nurture an inclusive school in that locality. Secondly it assesses the resources available within schools and identifies their strengths and weaknesses in order to make the school more inclusive. This knowledge will help in the selection of schools in which inclusive education will first be introduced. This data also serves as a baseline against which progress can be measured (see Chapter 11). We provide examples of tools that can be used to collect the necessary information.

This chapter is especially relevant to policy-makers in education, health and community services and those charged with the planning and delivery of new styles of service. It should also prove helpful to personnel involved in undertaking feasibility studies.

Key Learning Messages

- Feasibility studies are worth undertaking as they help you to gain an insight into the attitudes among teachers, families and the community towards children with disabilities and their education.

- Feasibility studies create awareness around Inclusive Education and help to identify allies in taking forward this idea.

- You will discover some of the possible pit-falls that may need to be addressed by your planning of an implementation strategy.

- You will gain an insight into the resources that are available in local schools and which may be needed.

- The feasibility study will assist you in drawing up priorities for action at a local school level as well as those that apply across most schools.

- By consulting with local schools and communities, the foundations of the participatory approach are being laid.

Preparing for a Feasibility Study

As explained in chapter 1, the feasibility study will follow on from other key steps in developing an inclusive education strategy. The actual form of these will vary according to the circumstances in each country but at a minimum they should include the following.

- The process requires an orientation workshop to policy makers and the constituting of a steering committee and perhaps specific project groups. The workshop should give an account of the inclusive education strategy, the importance of in-service teacher training, brief explanation of different disabilities and how to plan for teaching children with different abilities in one classroom.

- A national steering committee should be formed comprising representatives from different sectors; such as head teachers and teachers in regular schools, special educators from different areas of disabilities, representatives of parent organisations, NGOs of and for different disability organisations, health, social welfare and CBR personnel. Other educational personnel can be invited as needed such as curriculum development, examination departments and the inspectorate. Staff from relevant university departments and teacher training colleges could also be asked. The reason for this participatory approach is that it promotes ownership of the endeavour. All people who have been part of the process will proudly identify themselves with the initiative and do their best to sustain it. The Steering Group should be chaired by a senior official in the Ministry of Education.

- An inclusive education team should be established within the Ministry. This should consist of seconded teachers who have deep experience of educating children with special needs and a commitment to working inclusively. The leadership of this team is especially important. International donors may sponsor the participation of an international expert, as happened with Lilian Mariga.

Once these three elements are in place, the national steering committee and the inclusive education team can start to plan the proposed feasibility study. Their knowledge and experience will help to determine the range of information that needs to be gathered; the localities that might be targeted and the methods to be used in the study.

The people to carry out the study will probably be selected and trained by the Ministry of Education, although the leadership for this may have to come from a person with expertise in inclusive education, as happened in Lesotho and Zanzibar with Lilian Mariga's secondment.

Conducting a Feasibility Study

In this section we outline the content of a training session that prepares personnel to undertake a feasibility study of schools. More detailed work will need to be done in order to finalise the procedures to be used locally but this can follow on from the orientation that this Unit aims to provide.

Aims of a feasibility study

The objectives of the feasibility study could include the following:

- To establish whether there are children with disabilities already attending the regular schools.

- To investigate the attitudes of teachers, pupils, parents and community leaders towards inclusive education.

- To establish and assess whether there are resources such as learning materials, human resources and finances available to support children with special needs.

- To establish how conducive the environment is for children with physical and sensory impairments e.g. accessibility to classrooms and toilets.

- To assist in promoting awareness of inclusive education to all stake holders within education and the community at large.

IDEAS FOR COMMUNICATING THE MESSAGES

- Invite participants to identify other reasons as to why a feasibility study would be useful.
- Ask them to identify discuss which reasons should have priority.

Undertaking the feasibility study: An overview

An early decision has to be made about the people who will conduct the study. In the three African countries, these were mainly education personnel either based in the Ministry or experienced head teachers and teachers who were seconded from the Ministry to undertake the feasibility study. It was important that schools perceived the team as people with experience and authority. However, this was also a means of local persons taking ownership of the programme and learning from one another.

A team of four visited each school and spent one day collecting the information. This not only divided up the workload but enabled the team to share their perceptions with one another.

The total number of people recruited to the teams will depend on the number of schools to be included in the feasibility study. In Zanzibar, 12 people were trained to conduct the feasibility study. They were grouped by location so that a team could be allocated to one geographical area. Having a pool of trained persons also meant that people could be substituted if a person became unavailable for the school visit.

The Ministry of Education selected the schools to be included in the feasibility study. A range of schools were included such as those of various enrolments, urban versus rural schools. The head teachers of the prospective schools were contacted to establish whether they were interested in this new approach; what their feeling was towards Inclusive education and if they will cooperate when the team carrying out the feasibility study visited their school. It was important that the head teachers did not feel this new approach was being imposed on them but rather they had a choice of participating in testing it out.

If the Head Teacher was agreeable, a date for the visit was agreed and the programme for the visit outlined. The Head Teacher was asked to identify community personnel and parents who would be invited to the school to meet the team.

Prior to the visit, the instruments to be used by the people conducting the study should be designed, tabled and agreed upon with the National Steering Group. These are described in more detail below.

SUMMARY PROGRAMME FOR THE SCHOOL VISIT

- Meeting with Head Teacher to finalise programme for the visit.
- Meeting with teachers from a range of classes.
- Meeting with parents; especially those whose children have disabilities attending the school.
- Observing and inspecting the school facilities.
- Addressing pupils at school assembly to explain Inclusive Education.
- Visiting the village to assess distances, terrain, distances pupils have to walk.
- Meeting with community leaders and health personnel.
- Meeting with Head teacher and senior teachers to discuss Inclusive Education and their participation in the programme.
- Discussion among the team about their main findings and recommendations.

The selected teams of persons who would be gathering the information need to have training on how to use the questionnaires, on approaching the different groups, and on how to record and compile the collected information. After these training sessions, the team members have to be tested in the field by the study directors to assess how they ask the formulated questions and ensuring they are correctly documenting the responses. These initial trials of information gathering will also assist in refining the questionnaires and in deciding the time frame for the study.

The team would spend a full day in each school interviewing the identified personnel and observing and inspecting the school facilities. In addition the team also visited the villages to establish the community's perceptions of the programme and assess the facilities available (see Box on previous page). Team members shared these tasks among themselves.

Once all the interviewing is completed the information has to be analysed and reports written. Preferably an independent person should write the report of the findings that is submitted to the Steering Group set up by the Ministry of Education. Lilian Mariga did this in the three African countries.

IDEAS FOR COMMUNICATING THE MESSAGES

Part 1 of Programme 2: The Foundations of Inclusive Education in Zanzibar in the DVD *Inclusion in Action* (downloadable through YouTube – see p.11) give an overview of the feasibility study that was first undertaken in schools from across the country.

Examples of information gathered

The information gathered by the team was grouped into key themes as outlined below. The number of questions was kept to a minimum so as not to make the exercise too time-consuming.

1. Details of pupil enrolment

- What is the school enrolment?
- How many teachers are in the whole school?
- On average, how many students are in a class?
- Are they any students/youth with disabilities enrolled in the school?
- What type of disabilities are present in the classes? Female and male numbers are recorded.
- Is there a library with the materials for teaching pupils with disabilities?

The information was recorded on a pro forma such as this:

District	School	Number of Teachers	Total Enrolment	Hearing Impaired	Visually Impaired	Physically Impaired	Mentally Disabled	Others
			F – M	F – M	F – M	F – M	F – M	F – M

2. Ecological inventory of the school

The team checked the physical environment of the school and surroundings, notably accessibility of the classrooms and toilets. They looked for the following:

- Are there steps into classrooms – are doors wide enough for a wheel-chair?
- What types of toilets are at the school?
- Are the toilets and doors accessible?
- Are there water facilities at the school?
- Type of roads used by other students going to school?
- What is the average distance walked by students to school?
- Are there any recreation facilities at the school e.g. netball, football grounds, indoor games and other leisure and recreation facilities?

The information was summarised on a table such as the following:

Name of School	Classroom Access	Toilets	Water Resources	Roads/ Distance Walked	Recreation Facilities

3. Resources

Information was gathered on the resources available to the school.

- Have teachers experience of teaching students and youths with disabilities?
- What training have teachers had of teaching students with disabilities? Who provided the training?
- What resources are available to teachers to aid children's learning and their teaching?
- What finances does the school have for needed teaching materials?
- Is there an active Parent–Teacher Association?
- Does the community include youth with disabilities in leisure and recreation activities?
- What links does the school have with health services, CBR programmes, Disabled People's Organisations.

Again the information was summarised on a table such as the following:

Name of School	Teachers' Experience	Training for Teachers	Teaching Aids	PTA	Recreation Activities	Community Links

4. Attitudes of school and community personnel

The team had a dual function of both informing school personnel about Inclusive Education and of gauging their reactions to it. Hence they gave short presentations to groups of staff, students and parents about making schools more inclusive – why it was being considered and how it might happen. Afterwards they spoke to individual teachers or groups of students and parents and noted if their reactions were broadly positive, negative or unsure. They also asked various questions to ascertain topics of particular concern to them:

- Have you heard of Inclusive Education previously? How do you feel about your school becoming an Inclusive School? Would you support this new approach?
- What benefits are there to the disabled child and youth, to their family and society at large?
- Are there any problems or difficulties that might arise?
- Any ideas as to how they might be overcome?
- A similar approach was used in speaking with parents and community personnel but some additional questions were added:
- What is the relationship between school, parents and community members?
- How might these relationships be improved?

Summary tables were used to collate their reactions to Inclusive Education in terms of positive (P), negative (N) and unsure (U) responses.

Name of School	Head Teacher	Teachers	Students	Parents	Community Leaders	People with Disabilities
	P-N-U	P-N-U	P-N-U	P-N-U	P-N-U	P-N-U
	P-N-U	P-N-U	P-N-U	P-N-U	P-N-U	P-N-U
	P-N-U	P-N-U	P-N-U	P-N-U	P-N-U	P-N-U

A summary table was used to summarise the main benefits and issues that had been identified.

School	Benefits Identified	Possible Problems	Proposals

Please note: The above examples can be changed according to the information the particular country wants to establish. The Steering Group and the Team will decide on this but we would caution about trying to collect too much information at this stage. The aim is to gain a broad appreciation of how Inclusive Education is viewed. It is better to include a greater number of schools rather than spend more time with fewer schools.

Reporting the findings from the feasibility study

The information that is gathered needs to be brought together into a report that details the number and types of schools that were involved; their location; how people were selected for interview and the numbers of people interviewed. The findings can be presented either as summary tables as noted above or summarised by text (see example below). The team might also draft some recommendations and conclusions based on the findings.

The draft report can then be presented to the Steering Group for comment and approval before it is passed to the Ministry of Education and other interested parties represented in the Steering Group.

After tabling the feasibility study report to the key ministries, planning for the implementation of Inclusive Education can begin. The remaining chapters deal with this.

> IDEAS FOR DISCUSSING THE PRACTICALITIES OF UNDERTAKING A FEASIBILITY STUDY
> - How might teachers be encouraged to give their honest opinion rather than the answers they think the Team wants to hear.
> - How might parents views be obtained: e.g. through individual interviews or group meeting?
> - What community resources should the team check out?

Example of findings

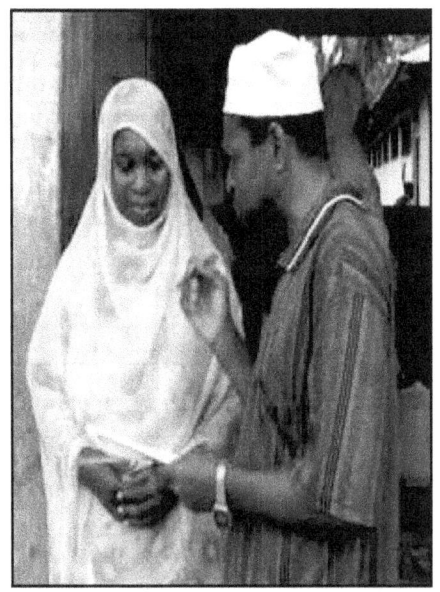

The results in the three countries, Lesotho, Zanzibar and Tanzania were broadly similar regarding attitudes to inclusive education and they were as follows:

- Although there was generally a positive attitude towards inclusive education, around one third of stake holders doubted if the approach would work. Hence a lot of educating and dissemination of information on the process of inclusive education was necessary.

- A small number of school heads were very negative and this affected the attitudes of teachers as well. However it was important to include these schools in the early stages of implementing Inclusive Education as a way of demonstrating that it can work even under initially unpromising conditions.

- Parents were also sceptical about the inclusive education approach because most of them had fears that their children will be abused, laughed at, and neglected. They also felt that their children will not have the individual attention they have in special education units. Some of the parents were still hiding children with disabilities. Hence parent education was an important strand in implementing Inclusive education.

- Some teachers felt it would be a lot of work, that they will not meet the syllabus, they felt inclusion will lower their standards and the pass rate will be affected. Hence a great deal of effort had to be put into changing teacher's perceptions mainly through using experienced teachers as trainers of others.

- Particular resistance came from staff serving in special schools, centres and units. These felt their jobs would be taken over, and therefore defended their domains. The inclusive education implementers convinced them that they were important personal to the process and they played a very important role in the training of parents and teachers. This gave them assurance and most of them went on to develop their studies further by taking diplomas and degrees related to special educational needs.

- The other students were positive, they were the only ones who welcomed the approach, because they felt the students with disabilities were their brothers and sisters, and they all lived together. Hence student representatives were included in the School Committees set up for Inclusive Education and the use of peer-mentoring approaches was encouraged.

- Policy makers within education initially felt that the process was not going to work; Inclusive Education would be expensive and time consuming. Through setting up of steering and planning committees and by sharing of information on an ongoing basis, they finally supported the process fully and formulated inclusive policies.

- The feasibility study also identified how poorly resourced the schools were to meet the needs of their pupils and the lack of experience and training of teachers in special needs. The number of specialist trained teachers was very limited. Contacts with parents and communities were generally limited although better contacts were welcomed.

These barriers could be used as an argument for saying that Inclusive Education could not be successfully implemented. Alternatively they could be used to say that Inclusive Education must be implemented because by so doing all children would receive an improved education. It was the latter argument that prevailed.

Implementing an Inclusive Education Programme

The feasibility study assisted the drawing up of plans for the implementation of Inclusive Education nationally. However an early decision was to do this on an incremental basis by targeting groups of schools at a time. The first batch of around 20 schools were known as 'pilot schools' and in a sense, these schools formed another type of feasibility study.

The pilot schools were deliberately selected to include:

- Schools that were attempting to include children with disabilities.

- Schools that were positive to the initiative but had no students with disabilities enrolled.

- Schools that were negative to the idea.

- Schools that were neutral to the concept of inclusion.

In the remaining chapters we will describe the range of initiatives that were first tried out in the pilot schools so that lessons could be learnt and adaptations made before the programme was rolled out to further schools. Hence it was especially important to ensure that the pilot schools represented the range of reactions that would arise.

In chapters 1 and 2 we have given an overview of the various actions that are required when it comes to implementing Inclusive Education. In the following chapters we examine certain core issues in more detail: notably

- Preparing teachers (Chapter 8).

- Supporting pupils to learn (Chapter 9).

- Managing Inclusive classrooms (Chapter 10).

- Future Challenges (Chapter 11).

Two big lessons stand out when it comes to implementation.

- There is no one approach that is guaranteed to work with all schools. Rather you have to be flexible and adapt your advice and guidance to local situations. Equally you have to be open to new ideas and approaches that others have come up with.

- Schools and communities have to find their own solutions and at their own pace. This can be frustrating for those wishing to make changes happen nationally and speedily but to impose changes can mean it never really takes root and can easily wither.

IDEAS FOR COMMUNICATING THE MESSAGES

Part 2 of Programme 2 The Foundations of Inclusive Education in Zanzibar in the DVD *Inclusion in Action* (downloadable through YouTube – see p.11) describes the work undertaken in the 20 pilot schools to set up inclusive education. This illustrates many of the points made in this chapter and later chapters.

CHAPTER 8:
Preparing Teachers

Teacher education is the key to the effective implementation of inclusive education as its success is largely dependent on the attitudes and skills of teachers. Most will have little previous experience of teaching children with disabilities and may feel that they will not be able to cope with the extra demands that will be placed on them. But it would be a mistake to think that teachers alone can make schools inclusive. Rather it is important to recognise that reconstructing schools challenges the status quo of schooling and teacher education. This has to happen at all levels.

- At a political level, it raises questions to those who create and administer policy.

- At a school level, it tests the commitment of Boards of Management and head teachers.

- At a professional level, it presents challenges to individual teachers and those involved in their education and training.

Specifically it requires many to suspend their existing beliefs and assumptions about the origins and nature of educational difficulties in order to consider alternative perspectives. Instead of the traditional search for specialist techniques that can be used to ameliorate the learning difficulties of an individual pupil, the focus must be on finding ways of creating the conditions that will remove the barriers pupils face in learning and ways of facilitating and supporting the learning of all children.

These changes of perspective are not easy to achieve. Teaching is a demanding and intensive activity leaving little time for reflection. Furthermore the attitudes of teachers are often deeply rooted, having been established through the process of professionalising that occurs during initial training and, perhaps even more significantly within the workplace.

Our aim in educating teachers is for them to become confident of their own abilities; to learn from their experiences and emphasise social processes and resources as a means of facilitating their professional development. Hence this Unit can be used to open up discussion among educational personnel about the training opportunities proved for teachers in order to assist them in making their schools more inclusive.

Teacher education about Inclusive Education

Although inclusive education needs to feature in all initial teacher training, the existing teaching workforce would benefit from in-service training with respect to inclusive education as indeed would other practitioners across many disciplines and professionals, notably doctors, therapists, psychologists and social workers.

Teachers need to be helped to develop a wider perspective to educational difficulties and approaches to teaching in an inclusive classroom. What is needed is developing teachers so that they can adjust education in line with the children's learning. Because a successful inclusive classroom provides the conditions for all children's learning, so teacher development must address contextual matters in order to create the conditions that facilitate the learning of all students.

Inclusive education can help teachers to reach new understanding about the important issues in society; such as parents as partners in education. Teachers may be inclined to think of some parents as 'enemies' but with training and exposure to parents, they came to realise that they were on their side and that they want the best for the children. Likewise teachers who blamed children for their bad behaviours, with training they recognised that the problems could stem from teachers and how the classroom was organised.

In this chapter we describe approaches that have proved successful in preparing African teachers for Inclusive Education. However further work and future research should be broadened to assist in evaluating the most effective and efficient means of changing attitudes, gathering knowledge and enhancing skills amongst all stake holders - including teachers - and in integrating their efforts in bringing about shifts in culture and practices. There is no easy, simple way of doing this. How it is undertaken is very much dependent on each country's resources and existing policies. Change has to come from within.

We describe two main methods of preparing teachers.

- The provision of in-service training courses
- The preparation of training manuals and accompanying video programmes.

We also note the value of schools learning from one another and how this can be encouraged.

Proposals were also drawn up for the content of a module on Inclusive Education that could be used in initial teacher-training. This drew on the experiences gained in delivering the in-service courses and was done in consultation with staff from the teacher training colleges. Details are available on request.

Key Learning Messages

- Teacher education needs to embrace attitudes, knowledge, understanding and skills.
- It should equip teachers in devising and implementing individual education plans and in managing classrooms.
- It should enable teachers to work in partnership with families and other stakeholders in the community.
- Training should be largely school-based and applicable to the local situation in which teachers work.
- A range of personnel can be recruited, trained and deployed as teacher educators, notably experienced teachers within mainstream schools and teachers with specialist training in disabilities.
- Schools should be encouraged to learn from one another. Those with more experience of inclusive education can share their expertise with other schools.

Theme 1: Providing In-service Teacher Education

The training needs of teachers were identified in the feasibility studies that were undertaken (see Chapter 7) as well as drawing on experience from other countries.

With guidance from the National Steering Committee, the inclusive education team set up by the Ministry of Education in each country were involved in drawing up and delivering the in-service education programme.

This took various forms. An awareness raising workshop on Inclusive Education was run for policy makers from Ministry of Education and Ministry of Health as well as the Head of Departments in Education such as curriculum and examination boards. This workshop was also repeated for managers and staff in INGOs and DPOs. Variations of this workshop were used to introduce teachers and parents to Inclusive Education. These workshops drew on the content described in chapters 1 and 2.

An in-service course on Inclusive Education was devised for teachers in participating schools. The participants were selected teachers from the schools involved in the pilot programme and their head teachers. Local inspectors and subject resource teachers who were involved with the schools were also invited to attend. The number of persons attending depended on the total of primary schools selected for the piloting of the Inclusive Education Programme. In Lesotho, the pilot covered 10 schools with seven teachers attending from each school initially whereas Zanzibar had 20 piloting schools and upwards of 140 teachers attended for in-service training.

The course tutors were mainly staff working in the Inclusive Education Team. In addition invited lecturers came from the Ministry of Education, special educators, therapists and other specialists from Ministry of Health, CBR programmes and parents.

The meetings were conducted at the Teacher training college in Lesotho and Zanzibar. The training course took place over two weeks during the school holiday break. In addition special sessions lasting one week were devoted to Braille and Sign Language training, again during school breaks. Some follow-up workshops were held in schools during monitoring and follow-up visits to revise areas in which teachers were having difficulties, e.g. undertaking assessments and Individual Education Programme (IEP). In all the in-service training took place over 18 months. The course content is described below.

An international NGO (Save the Children UK in Lesotho and NFU in Zanzibar) funded the costs of the in-service training; including the teacher's upkeep in residences, transport, food, accommodation and out of pocket allowances for teaches and lectures.

Teachers as trainers

In Lesotho and Zanzibar, selected teachers were sent on specialist training courses relating to particular disability conditions in neighbouring countries. On their return, they were then expected to provide training courses for other teachers and were released from their schools to do so. This proved to be a cost-effective means of providing more sustainable training opportunities to local teachers because these trained teachers were available to give ongoing guidance and support to schools instead of the Ministries hiring tutors from other countries. However, the Ministries of Education in both countries sourced funds for their training from other donor agencies because of limited budgets.

This model was also extended to those teachers who were attending the inservice training courses. They were encouraged to provide briefing sessions in their local schools to keep their colleagues informed about the new learning they had acquired.

Short courses and workshops

Shorter courses were also provided on specific topics as requested by teachers; for example courses on sign language. These took place after school for teachers within that school or else a one or two day workshop for a group of teachers from neighbouring schools. These were lead by the Inclusive Education Team and the teachers who had been trained in specific areas.

Further learning opportunities

Further opportunities can also be provided to widen teacher's education and experience of inclusive education. These include:

- Group teaching: a less experienced teacher can work alongside a more experienced one.

- Study visits: teachers can visit other schools to observe lessons and discuss common issues.

- A guest speaker can be invited to talk on or advise on a topic that teachers are not familiar with.

- Peer support groups: A group of teachers within a school may meet regularly for a short period to discuss issues of common concern and get ideas from one another.

Teachers should be aware that inclusive education is hard work. How well they survive the pitfalls and challenges depends on their success in coming to terms with themselves as effective teachers. During any of these training opportunities, they should learn to examine their personal successes, failures and attitudes so that they learn and grow.

IDEAS FOR REFLECTING ON TEACHER EDUCATION

- Participants could reflect on the training opportunities that are presently available in their country and identify if they might be used to further teachers' understanding of Inclusive Education.
- Who are the persons who can act as tutors on teacher training courses? How can they be prepared to undertake this work?

In-service course on Inclusive Education

As an example, we have outlined the aims and content of the courses used in Zanzibar and Lesotho. This can be used as the basis for similar courses in other countries or parts might be presented in the form of short courses or workshops. See Table 8.1.

The main aims of the course were:

- To help teachers to prepare the class for including those with disabilities and by informing other students about disabling conditions and how they can assist them.

- To identify appropriate learning objectives and make educational plans.

- To use appropriate teaching methods and aids according to the learner's needs.
- To adapt the curriculum and teaching strategies so that all learners benefit.
- To adapt and manage the classroom to maximise children's opportunities for learning.
- To work in partnership with parents, other professionals and community personnel.

The table below summarises the course content.

TABLE 8.1: INSERVICE COURSE CONTENT
Introduction
Current trends of inclusion and Inclusive education in UN and international documents
Causes of learning disabilities and some disabilities/handicaps
Policies and services available in the country
Psychological and social aspects of children with learning disabilities
Psychological effects on parents
Psychological effects on learners with handicaps
Psychological effects on professionals, communities and their attitudes
General principles of learning
Principles of inclusion
Assessing children strengths and difficulties
Goal planning
Curriculum and its components
Using interaction methods
Teaching strategies
Behaviour problems and how to manage them
Knowledge of different disabilities
Education of learners with hearing impairment
Causes of hearing impairments
Screening and use of hearing aids
Education of people who are deaf/hearing impaired
Curriculum and instructional methods
Education of learners with visual impairment/total blindness
Causes of blindness
Types of visual impairments
Screening and use of vision aids
Instructional methods – IT and Braille
Education of learners with Intellectual disabilities
Definitions and causes of intellectual disabilities
Identification and assessment
Planning of IEPs
Instructional methods
Behaviour problems and modification
The role of family and community in education
Extra-curricular
Counselling parents of children with disabilities
Activities of daily living
Medical aspects
Vocational training
Leisure and recreation

Teaching/Learning procedures

A variety of teaching and learning procedures were used during the course. These included:

- Lectures
- Discussions
- Group work
- Role play
- Demonstrations
- Assignments
- Visual aids
- Case studies
- Practicum
- Child to child
- School home programmes

Evaluation

Verbal and written feedback was obtained from the course participants as a means of evaluating the value of the course to them and of adjusting the content and delivery to better meet their needs. However, participants were very positive. In addition course participants were expected to undertake practical activities within their school and classroom to facilitate the application of the training they had received.

Teachers in both Lesotho and Zanzibar reported that the enrolment of student with learning difficulties and those with disabilities was very high. Teachers also said the in-service training had helped them, they enjoyed teaching more, they further said the programme helped and equipped them with different teaching techniques that they were also able to use with the so called "normal pupils". The teachers reported that they stayed on at school after hours to plan together. They also said that having knowledge on assessing pupils' strengths and weakness helped them to understand the students' needs individually.

The courses were also supplemented by written handouts which in time were collated into training manuals that were printed and distributed to schools.

Theme 2: Training Manuals for Teachers

The production of training manuals for teachers was a milestone in the three countries. Although the relevant services providers had booklets on physical disabilities and visual impairment, very little was done in the areas of intellectual and hearing impairment. It is also important that resource materials should address the needs of the target groups and they should be relevant to the situation in that particular country. Materials used in other countries should not be imposed but carefully read and examined and reproduced to address the cultural norms.

A multidisciplinary team was recruited to review and proof read the draft manuals prepared by the Inclusive Education Team. This consisted of parents, regular schoolteacher, teachers' union representative, and specialist teachers with expertise in four main types of disabilities, a curriculum developer, examination board representative, a member of staff from the teacher's training college, pre-school teachers and members of disabled people's organisations.

The primary aim was to give teachers a better understanding of the difficulties which pupils with disabilities experience in learning and to encourage a uniform approach within and across schools to the teaching strategies and curriculum adaptations that are needed.

In Lesotho and Zanzibar, the pack of resource materials consisted of:

- A teacher guide to inclusive education
- A booklet on assessments
- Manuals in four areas of disabilities – physical, visual, intellectual and hearing
- The content of the in-service course

In Zanzibar, a course outline was also developed on training in life-skills and vocational skills that could be used with older learners and school leavers.

Once the draft manuals were approved by the multi-disciplinary team, the next step was to field test them. This was done through the in-service training courses over a period of eighteen months during which teachers gave feedback as to their appropriateness.

The evaluation results were shared with the National Steering Group and presented to the Ministry. Approval was then given for the printing of the manuals for use in future training courses – both in-service and pre-service courses.

Audio-Visual Materials

In Lesotho and Zanzibar a series of video programmes were made to illustrate inclusive education in practice (see Table 8.2). Video has a number of advantages as a teaching medium (Holloway et al., 1999). It is:

- **Visual:** Viewers can see new ideas and approaches in action. A variety of activities can be quickly displayed and viewers can watch the sequences a number of times to reinforce their learning.
- **Culturally Appropriate:** Local scenes depict the viewer's reality and emphasise that the messages are appropriate to the culture and that they are already being applied there.
- **Local Languages:** If necessary, commentaries in local languages can be dubbed on to the video-programmes; thereby making training more accessible to everyone.
- **Easily Transportable:** Video cassettes or DVDs can be easily taken or sent to any places which have video playback equipment. This is becoming more readily available throughout the world. Recorders and televisions can be battery operated.

- **Easily Repeated:** The video programmes can be easily repeated with different groups of parents or community workers; and although such programmes are time-intensive to produce, they are very time-efficient thereafter.

- **Enhanced Status:** Portraying families and children with disabilities on video can enhance their status within the community as the programmes focus on what the people with disabilities can do for themselves.

- **Proven Effectiveness:** Research in both developed and developing countries has demonstrated the effectiveness of this method of training with families and staff. In developed countries, video-based training is expanding rapidly in education and in the business world. DVDs can now be downloaded over the Internet and played through computers as well as on DVD or video players.

TABLE 8.2: CONTENT OF VIDEO PROGRAMMES MADE IN LESOTHO
Part 1: Foundations of Inclusive Education
1. Inclusive education history for Lesotho
2. Changing attitudes in disability
3. Screening for disabilities
Part 2: Common impairments
1. Overcoming visual impairments'
2. Overcoming hearing impairments
3. Overcoming physical disabilities
4. Overcoming intellectual disabilities
Part 3: Responding to diversity in classrooms
1. Preparing teachers to adapt to the curriculum in reading, writing and number concepts
2. Responding to differences in classrooms
Part 4: Supporting Inclusive Education
1. Training manuals for communities
2. Parent training
3. Early identification and intervention
4. Community education on disability issues
5. Self-help skills and pre-vocation skills

The video programmes produced in Lesotho give an overall account of the whole process of making schools more Inclusive. All the recordings were made on location in schools, communities and family homes around the country. The 14 programmes were grouped into four parts and the content is summarised in Table 8.2. Details are available from Eenet: http://www.eenet.org.uk/resources/docs/video.pdf

The video programmes were used as part of the in-service training courses. They were also made available to teachers to use when they were training other teachers or groups such as parents. They were especially valuable when illustrating practical strategies that can be used in schools. Selected programmes were used in awareness sessions with other groups such as parents and community representatives.

A range of other ready-made video programmes are available – see the References section at the end of the book. However as video cameras reduce in price and editing is now possible through computers, it may be possible for schools and teachers to make their own video programmes for use in staff training.

Theme 3: Schools Learning from One Another

The challenge of creating education for ALL pupils in a township or rural area cannot be done by one school in isolation. Rather it requires the active co-operation and participation of all the schools within a district – pre-school, primary and secondary. This is essential to ensure continuity in the education of children with special needs. Much good work will be undone if a pupil has to transfer schools and the receiving school is not prepared to adapt to their needs.

Co-operation among schools is even more crucial if special schools are located in the district. When ordinary and special schools work together, the pupils and teachers in both types of schools will gain. However the tradition in many countries is that each school is expected to be self-sufficient with little contact and communication occurring between teachers and pupils beyond competitive games!

The educational authorities of course should give a lead in bringing school together. But if this is not forthcoming, then teachers, and more especially head teachers, can get things moving.

Here are some ideas that are emerging from our work to foster partnerships between schools in supporting each other's efforts towards inclusive education.

- The head teachers of the schools and representatives of the School Board of Management meet at least once a year to review issues of common concern. This could include admission of children with special needs; access to buildings and equipment; training of staff and support for teachers and children.

- Likewise, teachers can visit each other's schools to learn about the initiatives they have taken in their classroom to include special needs children.

- The schools might try to establish in their district a shared resource centre of teaching aids and equipment; books, magazines and video programmes that teachers and families can use. It would ideal if this was linked to a local teacher education institute as happened on Pemba in Zanzibar.

- Teachers may be seconded to another school for a period of time. For example, a teacher from a special school may go to a neighbouring primary school to assist the staff there with particular pupils. This could happen for a period of time – for two weeks – or one day a week for a term. Likewise, teachers from the ordinary school could be seconded to the special school or unit.

- In some countries, the education authorities have provided 'resource' teachers to assist pupils with special needs. They may cover a number of schools. These resource teachers could convene teachers' meetings; arrange for teacher exchanges and organise training inputs for groups of staff drawn from all the schools for which they have responsibility.

- A 'Working ' group of teachers drawn from all the local schools can be convened to work on topics of mutual interest in special needs education; such as curricula adaptations, teaching methods and assessing children's learning. These working groups should have a specific focus and be time-limited. The product can be shared with all schools. This means that work gets done which one school could not do on its own but it also produces shared policies and procedures across the schools.

- If a teacher from one school attends a training course on special needs; on their return they could become a resource for the teachers in other schools in the district; for example by speaking at staff meetings or at parent meetings or they might organise training inputs for local teachers.

- Groups of schools within an area might invite local 'experts' in special education needs to present training workshops for all their staff. They may be found in teacher training colleges, universities, Ministry of Education or non-governmental organisations (NGOs). By combining with other schools, such events will attract reasonable numbers of participants and once again, networks are built among teachers.

- Pupil exchanges can also be encouraged between those in special and mainstream schools. This can take many forms: visiting for social events such as concerts and sharing lessons in particular subjects – such as art, P.E., music. Schools that are physically close could base a class in each other's premises to increase the informal contacts pupils have with one another. Also particular children with special needs may attend the ordinary school for some or nearly all of their lessons. These sorts of arrangements can be reviewed as the children's needs change. The child may come to spend more or less time in one or other setting.

Concluding comment

The main resource in making inclusive schools a reality are teachers. Hence their concerns and needs must be actively addressed. There are many pressures on schools and teacher morale can be low. Hence inspirational leadership is needed that stresses their contribution in building strong communities and nations. In this respect, the role of head teachers is crucial and worldwide is acknowledged as the key to transforming schools.

IDEAS FOR COMMUNICATING THE MESSAGES

Programme 4: Support for Teachers in the DVD *Inclusion in Action* (which is also downloadable through YouTube, see p.11) illustrates the support provided to teachers in Zanzibar including the role of the Inclusive Education Unit in the Ministry and the provision of in-service training courses for teachers.

CHAPTER 9:
Supporting Pupils to Learn

Children with disabilities find it harder to learn but they can learn. The good news is that teachers have found many ways of overcoming the difficulties they experience. In this chapter we outline the approaches African teachers used in their classrooms to help the pupils with special needs. Of course these same approaches also proved beneficial to other pupils who did not have an identified disability but who found school work difficult.

In the beginning the teachers had to put in some extra work to get started but once their expertise and confidence grew, these adaptations to their usual practice became easier to make.

There are many resources available to help teachers respond to the needs of children with learning difficulties. We have listed these at the end of the book. Our aim in this chapter is to identify key strategies that have proved effective across a range of disabling conditions and which teachers could implement in their classrooms without needing extra money or special equipment. As we outlined in Chapter 8, teachers need opportunities to be trained in these new approaches, either through school-based workshops, teacher training courses or by visiting and observing practice in other schools. Hence this chapter summarises the content that could be covered in more detail through a range of workshops around the theme of supporting pupil's learning.

The two main messages are simply stated.

- Teachers should focus on the particular needs of the individual pupil. This philosophy of one child at a time makes the whole process of inclusion much more manageable.

- Teachers should enlist the support of others to assist and advise them such as other teachers and parents. This too takes the pressures off teachers.

Key Learning Messages

- Teachers need to identify the particular barriers that children experience in learning. This means undertaking assessments of the child's difficulties with the aim of reducing or wherever possible removing obstacles to learning.

- Teachers should draw up a plan as to how to overcome these difficulties – this is known as an Individual Education Plan (IEP).

- Teachers can use various strategies to help children to learn. These structured teaching approaches require teachers to change the way they teach individual children or small groups of children.

The main themes in this training unit

This unit has five main themes:

- We focus on importance of teacher communication in classrooms and especially with learners who may have communication difficulties.

- We explain how teachers can undertake assessments of the child to determine their particular difficulties.

- We stress the importance of having an Individual Education Plan (IEP) for the learner.

- We describe structured teaching strategies that have proved helpful in overcoming learning difficulties.

- We outline how teachers can get extra help so that a pupil with special needs get individual attention.

Theme 1: Communication

It is obvious that teachers need to make their communication very clear when teaching. But this is even more important if there is a learner with special needs in the class as he or she may experience extra difficulties in hearing or understanding what the teachers says and what is expected of them. But communication is more than talking. We also communicate visually and by actions (see Box). A good communicator always uses various channels or ways to communicate and repeats essential content by using different activities.

> **HUMANS COMMUNICATE THROUGH...**
> - Speech
> - Gestures – pointing and miming actions
> - Facial expression – to indicate when you are pleased, cross, puzzled
> - Eye gaze – to indicate who you want to communicate with; or draw people's attention to objects
> - Pictures and symbols
> - Reading and writing
> - Sign languages – such as those used by deaf people
> - Singing, acting, dancing and touching

Teachers should:

- Be clearly seen by all the pupils – stand rather than sit at the desk.
- Stand closer to children with special needs so it is easier for them to hear you and to see your gestures.
- Talk clearly and project your voice (slightly raised) but not shouting.
- Keep the words simple and the sentences short.
- Alert the pupils to important messages: "listen carefully" – and make eye contact with them if it is culturally appropriate.
- Repeat important messages.
- Use gestures and facial expressions alongside language to get your meaning across. These methods are especially useful when organising or controlling the class. But they should also be used when explaining and teaching.
- Check with the pupils who may have problems that they have understood. Ask them to repeat what you have said or to say in their own words what you have told them.
- Augment your verbal communication with pictures, drawings and writing. This can be done on a chalkboard for the whole class or on a slate or paper for an individual learner.
- Encourage the children to indicate if they have not understood by raising their hands and asking you questions. They should also do this when they do not understand what other pupils have said.

- If you cannot make out what the learner is saying, encourage the child to show you or to gesture.
- You may find that classmates or brothers and sisters of the child are able to tell you what the child is trying to communicate. Get their help.

Communication aids

Individual pupils can benefit from communication aids according to their particular needs.

These include:

- **Hearing aids:** for those who have been assessed as having a hearing impairment (see next theme).
- **Picture boards:** made up of photographs, drawing or symbols. Teachers and pupils can point to the pictures as a means of communicating.
- **Sign language and finger spelling:** Teachers can easily learn the basics of sign language. Although intended for children with severe hearing impairments sign language can help hearing children who have difficulties with speaking and learning language. In some African schools, all the class took part in sign language lessons so that they too can communicate with their peers. Contact your National Association for Deaf Persons for information about the training courses they run.
- Modern technology provides other communication aids such as computers that can speak text for blind students.

> **IDEAS FOR COMMUNICATING THE MESSAGES**
>
> Invite a communication specialist such as a speech and language therapist to provide a workshop on enhancing communication in the classroom. This would include a demonstration of communication aids and how they can be made by teachers and parents.

Theme 2: Assessing Children's Difficulties

Learners with special educational needs are a very varied group. Some have sensory or physical disabilities; others may have intellectual or behavioural difficulties. Some pupils may have multiple difficulties. It is important for teachers to identify each child's particular difficulties. Inadequate and inaccurate assessment can lead to inappropriate decisions. To cite one example, children may be wrongfully regarded as intellectually disabled when in fact their difficulties in learning may be mainly due to hearing impairment. In many societies, educational resources may be denied the child who is considered intellectually disabled.

Educational assessment has been defined as a diagnosis of educational strengths, weakness and needs, defining a child's current level of functioning and leading to the appropriate placement and informing instructional objectives and activities. This means teachers should assess children in the following areas of development.

- **Mobility:** how the student moves from place to place and their need for assistance in moving about all areas of the school including use of toilets.

- **Sensory difficulties:** checking for hearing and vision problems.

- **Physical ability and limitations:** notably their use of hands - and any problems with sitting in chairs or on the floor.

- **Activities of daily living:** such as dressing, toileting and eating.

- **Language development:** understanding what is said to them as well as their level of expressive language.

- **Academic readiness:** for learning to read, write and number work.

- **Behaviour and emotions:** attention and concentration, their self-esteem, relationships with others.

Parents or other family members can be invited to take part in these assessments. This is a good way of checking if the child shows the same difficulties at home as well as in school.

Teachers might wish to undertake the assessments alongside a more experienced colleague or disability specialist. This will help them to become more proficient in undertaking assessments.

From the assessments which the teachers undertake, a profile can be drawn up of the child's strengths as well as their weaknesses. An individual educational plan can then be devised for the child (see later). This will aim to develop the child's strengths as well as plans for managing their weaknesses. The assessment will also give teachers ideas for the teaching approaches and methods that are best suited to the child.

However, teachers might also refer the child for a more thorough assessment. These referrals could be to a physical therapist, occupational therapist, speech and language therapist, psychologist, social workers or to the CBR programme if there is one in the locality. These referrals will hopefully give the child access to more specialised interventions, aids and appliances. Teachers should ask to be kept informed of the outcomes so that the child's IEP can be adjusted to incorporate the new information and advice.

Teachers should keep a record of their assessments. If these are repeated – for example at the end of each school term – they provide a measure of the child's progress.

Assessment tools

Many different tests have been devised to assess children's development. However these are developed for use in more affluent countries and many are not culturally appropriate for use in African societies. Rather we encourage teachers to conduct their own assessments based around observations of the child in structured and unstructured settings. Useful information can also be obtained from interviewing family members.

Teachers can learn a great deal from observing children in classrooms and around the school. However they need to know what to look out for. For example Box 1 gives a list of indicators that would suggest a child may have a problem with hearing. Their suspicions can be checked out by checking the child's hearing in a more structured way or by referring them for hearing assessments. Similar approaches can be used to assess vision difficulties (see References).

Box 1: Indications of hearing loss

- Inattention
- Turns head or ear towards speaker
- Fails to follow instructions especially in group setting
- Requests for questions or spoken words to be repeated
- Has speech problems
- Reluctant to volunteer in class or in group discussions
- Withdrawn behaviour
- Usually concentrates on speaker's face or mouth
- Cupping hand behind the ear
- Complains of ear-ache; discharge from ears

When undertaking structured assessments, it is very important that assessment is a pleasant experience for the child. When a child feels secure, appreciated and enjoys the activities he/she will be motivated and perform his/her best. This way you get the best impressions of the child's potential and needs. For an example, we found that bringing a child from a rural setting to an urban clinic for assessment does not give a true reflection of the child because the environment is not familiar and objects they are given are strange to them. It is better to observe children in familiar places and with people and objects they know.

Children can be assessed by asking them to undertake certain tasks. For example, Box 2 describes activities to assess children's fine motor control; arranged from easy to difficult. Developmental checklists like these are available on the Internet. However, researchers in Malawi have developed a tool for assessing early child development in culturally appropriate ways. Further details at: http://www.plosmedicine.org/article/info%3Adoi%2F10.1371%2Fjournal.pmed.1000273

Box 2: Assessing fine-motor control

- Reaches out and picks up small objects from the floor
- Turns pages of a book
- Picks up small objects (e.g. small piece of string) between finger and tip of thumb
- Scribbles in circles and straight lines
- Removes a screw-top from bottle
- Tries to cut with scissors
- Draws a man – showing head, legs and hand

Teachers should create a file for each child that can be used to record their observations. This can be shared with parents and passed on to other teachers when the child moves classes.

> **IDEAS FOR COMMUNICATING THE MESSAGES**
>
> Organise a workshop on school-based assessments. This would provide teachers with details of the range of assessments they could undertake and also give them the opportunity to practice them. The video made in Lesotho gives examples of teachers undertaking assessments.

Theme 3: Individual Education Plans

Every child is an individual. Hence teachers need to bear in the mind individual children's needs when planning and presenting their lessons. One way of doing this is by having an Individual Plan for each pupil with special needs. This is seen as good practice in many countries and is required by law in some countries.

- All pupils who are identified as having special needs should have an IEP started. If teachers are unsure, it is better to have an IEP than not to have one.

- For the primary school child, the plan identifies the specific teaching goals in the main curriculum areas, such as reading and number work. For secondary school pupils, their plan may also cover the different subject areas.

- Deciding on new learning objectives is not easy. These should not be too difficult that the child is discouraged, yet you need to challenge the child to learn new skills. Do not worry about getting it right first time. If the child quickly learns the goals you have selected, you can add others. Likewise if the goals prove too difficulty, see if you can break the task down into smaller steps and have the child work on these instead (see next section).

- The plan should also identify any special arrangements that have proved useful in helping the child to cope at school, such as seating position, use of aids and so on.

- If the child is receiving any special treatments – such as therapy- these goals should be added to the plan. This means there is one shared document that brings together all the steps taken to help the child's learning.

- The plans are best drawn up at the beginning of each school term. This is a time to review the child's progress in the past term as well as setting new goals. Hence the plans form a record of child's progress which can be shared with other teachers as the child moves through the school.

- The plan should be drawn up in consultation with the child's parents or carers. In this way, they can identify aspects of the curriculum that they feel is important for their child. It will also help to involve them in assisting the child at home. Parents should be given their own copy of the Plan. The IEP has been called the most effective communication aid between school and home.

- Head teachers should review all the IEPs when they are drawn up at the start of term and after they have been reviewed at the end of term. This will give them an opportunity to commend teachers on the progress the child has made but also helps them to identify changes they should make to the plan for the coming term.

- With older pupils, they can also be involved in the reviewing their plans. They may be able to share with you the difficulties they are finding with their schoolwork.

- When all the IEPs are reviewed across the school, head teachers will be able to identify the school's strengths in terms of meeting the children's educational needs but also identify areas of common difficulty. Training workshops can be provided on these topics.

Format of the IEP

There is no standard format for IEPs. Schools can develop the format that best suits their needs. It is best to keep the format simple – often one page is sufficient. A sample of an IEP form is given overleaf. After summarising information about the child, the form identifies up to five separate targets (those that are a priority for that learner). Each target should be specific and observable. The method of teaching is described for each target (the next section will describe available methods that teachers can use). The plan also details when the teaching will occur, who will assist the child and where the learning will take place. The final column can be used to record the child's progress and any changes made to the goal.

> #### IDEAS FOR COMMUNICATING THE MESSAGES
> Organise a series of action learning workshop for teachers on devising IEPs. Teachers should bring along their assessment folders on one or two pupils. In small groups they could brain-storm devising an IEP which they put into practice for a couple of weeks. They come back for a second session when they can share ideas for revising the IEPs in light of their experiences.

Theme 4: Assisting Students to Learn

Various strategies are available for teachers to use in helping pupils with learning difficulties. In this theme we can only briefly describe them but at the end of the book we list reference books and video programmes that will give much fuller information.

Creating a good learning environment

- Set aside an area of the classroom for the learner to use when you are focusing on specific teaching objectives.

- Keep the area free from distractions – not too noisy.

- Set up a time schedule so that the activities take place at the same times each day.

- Ensure any visual displays are at eye level and easily understood.

- Ensure the child is comfortably seated and any necessary aids are available (e.g. check the hearing aid is working).

Example of an Individual Education Plan

Student's name		Teacher	
Date of birth		Date IEP started	
Grade/class		Review date	
Main barriers to learning:			
Language of instruction/communication method:			
Aids/appliances used:			
Targets to be achieved	How they will be achieved	Who/when/where this will happen	Progress (NB continue overleaf)
1.			
2.			
3.			
4.			
5.			
Parent/carer contribution:			

- Select a time when the child is likely to be more alert. Children who take medication may become drowsy.

- One-to-one teaching (even for five minutes) may be best when introducing the child to a new activity (see Theme 5).

- Teaching groups of two or three children at a time also provides opportunities for peer-to-peer learning, especially if a more able student is included in the group.

Teachers' expectations

- Teachers should expect the child to be able to learn. If your pupil does not learn, it is your teaching that may need changing. Try another way!

- Give the learner plenty of encouragement. Use positive approaches when correcting mistakes. Don't shout or punish children. This rarely helps them to learn.

- Do not do things for them to cover up their disability. They have to try for themselves but you can adjust your demands if the task is proving too hard for them.

- Do not force learners to do something they are unwilling to do. Better to try something else and come back to the original task another time.

- For learners who have problems with concentration keep the sessions short. A number of short sessions per day are better than one long session. However over time you could increase the length of the sessions.

Teaching

- Setting the scene; getting the learner's attention. Find out what interests the learner and bring this into the lesson.

- Talk to the learner not at the learner. Maintain good eye contact. Use signs and gestures to make clear your meaning.

- Make learners aware of what you expect them to do – show them rather than tell them!

- Start with tasks you know they can do. Gradually make them more difficult. Be prepared to go back to simpler tasks so that they do become too discouraged.

- Children find it easier to work with objects rather than paper and pencil. Teachers can prepare teaching aids to assist the child. These will help learners to build interest in the subject and keep their attention. Examples are given in the video-programmes (see References).

- Correct inappropriate behaviours firmly and immediately (see Chapter 10 also).

- Reward learners when they accomplish the task.

Specific teaching techniques

There are various structured teaching techniques that can be used to assist students. You need to find those that work best with each student.

- Use modelling – show the learner what they have to do. The teachers or another student can model the skill for the learner so that he can see and understand.

- Break learning activities into small steps. For example, a child may not be able to recognise different coins. Rather than introducing all the coins at once, start with the two that are most different; then introduce another pair; then have them pick one from three coins and then from four coins and so on until the child has mastered the task. Teachers often use this step-by-step approach but perhaps with not with such small steps as described in this example.

- Chaining – when a task is broken down into small steps, the child is expected to first complete only one of the steps and the teacher does the others; then the child does two steps, then three steps and so on until they can do the whole task alone. For example, when putting on a T-shirt, the child has to put his head through the collar (step 1) the teacher does the rest. Then the child has to put his head in and one arm into the sleeve (two steps) and the teacher does the rest ... and so on. In this way, the child practices each step until they are successful at it.

- Use manual guidance – this means using your hands to guide the student through an activity such as controlling a pencil, drawing a straight line or learning to sand wood as in the photo.

- Use gestural prompts – such as signs and gestures to remind the child what to do.

- Use verbal prompts – they are verbal cues to guide the child as they undertake the task.

- Use rewards – such as praise and clapping – to keep the child motivated but also to let him or know they have done good work.

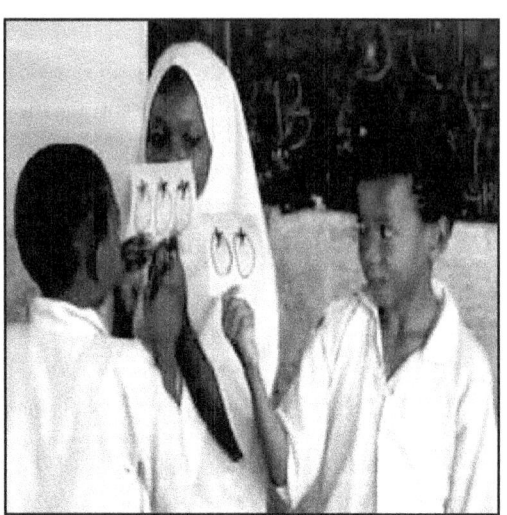

- Use a multi-sensory approaches – helping the child to learn through seeing, touching, hearing. Some students learn better through different modalities – vision and touch rather than listening and talking!

Common difficulties

Children with special needs often pose common difficulties for teachers. We list them here partly so that teachers know what to expect but also to have strategies prepared for dealing with them.

- **Slow pace of learning**. Learner finds it hard to pick up new concepts and ideas. They can find it hard to adapt to new or strange situations. Teacher should accept that they learn a little bit at a time.

- **Poor memory**. They may seem to have forgotten completely things they had learnt the day before. Constant repetition is needed to reinforce their learning.

- **Poor concentration**. He/she is able to do tasks for a short time and is easily distracted. It is best to have a short session with breaks in between.

- **Poor coordination and balance**. Learners can be clumsy and knock things over. Their hands and eyes do not work well together. Teachers should understand that they are not being deliberating naughty.

- **Speech and language**. Indeed all aspects of communication may be delayed. These include listening, hearing, speech, body language, conversation, thinking and understanding. Teachers need to find the methods of communication that works best for each learner. Always be patient with language; listen carefully, responding to the child so that you can develop their vocabulary and understanding of concepts.

- **Emotions**. The learners may not be able to hide their emotions. They can get cross and frustrated; they may cry and laugh readily. Others may be very shy and frightened. Teachers need to be very patient with emotions, watching and listening carefully for feelings he/she cannot put to words. Always try to improve the learners' esteem and confidence.

- **Inappropriate behaviours**. The learners may not be able to their behaviours and they are unconcerned about the effect they have on other people. For example, that pushing someone over may hurt them. (See next chapter for further details on managing behaviour).

- **Dangers**. The learners may do dangerous things – not realising the risk they are taking as their thoughts and reasoning powers are not fully developed. Teachers need to be extra vigilant and encourage other pupils to do likewise.

Teaching children who are slow learners is often very rewarding for teachers because every small step is a success and should be celebrated as such.

> IDEAS FOR COMMUNICATING THE MESSAGES
>
> Programme 5 in the DVD *Inclusion in Action* (also downloadable through YouTube, see p.11) contains model lessons that illustrate many of the teaching techniques described above. This can be used in training workshops with teachers. Teachers can be encouraged to share ideas for how they have adapted their teaching to meet the needs of particular children.

Theme 5: Individual Help

By definition, children with special needs need more support than do others in the class. They will therefore benefit more if the teaching is directed to their particular needs. But how can children get individual support? It is not easy but here are some ideas which teachers have found worked for them.

- When the class is working on an activity, the teacher may spend time with one or two children going over the main points of the lesson with them or helping them to get started on individual work related to the topic of the lesson.

- The children can be grouped by ability levels. The teacher can move from one to another to provide assistance tailored to their needs. This works well with reading and number work. Likewise in mixed ability groupings, more able children can assist the less-able children with their work.

- Children with special needs can be paired with a more able-student who can help them organise their work and assist them when they have completed their own work. This can benefit both pupils. This is known as 'peer-tutoring'.

- The teacher can keep the child back for 10 minutes at lunchtime to go over a lesson. The classroom is quiet then and the child has the teachers' complete attention.

- Two teachers can combine classes. One manages the whole group; while the other spends time doing individual or small group work with the special needs children.

- Older students in the school can be timetabled to assist with special needs students. This can form part of their social service courses.

- Volunteer helpers can be recruited to come into class to assist particular children. Family members, mothers or grandparents may be able and willing to do this. It may be for a limited time to help children settle into classes or to master the basics of certain subjects.

- Volunteers or staff working in Community-Based Rehabilitation projects are another source of individual support. They can be helpful when the child first starts at school as they will know the child and the family.

- If your school has access to resource teachers or specialist teachers, they can be called on to support the teachers in planning lessons and they could at times give individual support in the classroom.

- In more affluent countries, teacher's assistants are employed by the school to work in the classroom. Good communication and pre-planning between teachers and assistants is essential. Equally the presence of the assistant can inhibit the child with special needs from being an active participant in the class.

- At home family members can provide more individual attention than teachers can give in schools. Hence it is especially important that teachers engage with parents so that they can repeat the lessons at home.

IDEAS FOR COMMUNICATING THE MESSAGES

Brainstorm with teachers their ideas as to how children might receive individual support for their learning.

Concluding comment

The secret for successful inclusion is planning. Teachers need to be prepared in terms of having detailed knowledge about the learner, their chosen teaching goals, the strategies they will use to help the child learn, their preparation of the classroom and the teaching aids they will use. All this groundwork pays off in that the learners are then more easily managed within the class and more than that, they benefit from being there as they attain the goals set for them.

CHAPTER 10:
Managing Inclusive Classrooms

A key role of teachers is to ensure that the pupils in their class bond together as a group. This type of social capital has advantages for everyone. It makes the teacher's job easier as the class will be more manageable. There are fewer discipline problems. The pupils too will benefit as they help one another. They will enjoy coming to school and take pleasure in learning.

It is equally important that children with special needs are fully included within the class. This may not happen without deliberate planning on the part of the class teacher as well as the wider school community. This will mean changing existing practices. But that is the essence of inclusive practice: the removal of barriers that prevent children from learning rather than expecting the children to fit into practices that do not meet their needs.

We recognise the many demands placed on teachers in African schools. Large classes, inadequate classrooms, scarce teaching aids, to name but some. Yet we have been humbled by the creativity and resourcefulness of the teachers with whom we have worked in making their classes more inclusive. In this chapter we share with you the different strategies they have used to do this.

But perhaps more important than their actions is the mind-set that inspired them. They believed that:

- All learners are of equal value.
- The centred their teaching around their learners.
- They give positive feedback to children's work and behaviour.
- They do not embarrass learners when wrong answers are given.
- They ask the class for their opinion and whenever possible use their suggestions.
- By their example, they encourage pupils to be kind to one another and to help each other.
- They sensitise children about diversity and respect for one another's differences.

Wise head teachers applied this same mind-set in their dealings with teachers. They realised that when teachers felt valued, respected and trusted, they would be more likely to treat their pupils in a similar way.

Key Learning Messages

- Despite undoubted difficulties facing many African schools, teachers have managed to make their classrooms more inclusive and welcoming of learners with special needs.
- Teachers need the support of head teachers, Boards of Management and their colleagues for this to be successful.
- Various changes to classroom practices are possible. Teachers should focus first on those that are most necessary and more feasible.

The main themes in this training unit

This unit has five main themes with the common aim of helping teachers to create and manage inclusive classes. First, we examine ways of bonding the learners with special needs with other pupils in the class. Second, the layout of the class can be adapted to make teaching more manageable. Third we focus on the value of lesson planning and adapting the curriculum to the different levels of pupils. Fourth, we examine, opportunities for child-to-child learning within classes. Fifth, we outline strategies that teachers might use to manage disruptive behaviours.

Theme 1: Including Everyone

The value of inclusive education to pupils with special needs comes from mixing and sharing learning with other children in their classes. Teachers need to encourage this to happen as experience suggests that children with special needs can become isolated within classes and schools. This can lead them to disrupt lessons which may well result in them in being suspended and dropping out of school.

Teachers in the three countries used the approaches listed below to include pupils with special needs within their schools.

- They encouraged the enrolment of children from a young age. Then there are fewer differences with their peers; the children are more manageable when younger; they get into a routine that stays with them as they move through the school.

- Teachers explained to other pupils the reasons why some children cannot talk, why they behaved differently and so on. They did not shy away from acknowledging the children's impairments but they modeled how children might react with their disabled peers.

- Children who used assistive devices such as hearing aids or who depended on special equipment told the class about them and demonstrated how they were of help to them.

- Teachers encouraged children to 'befriend' pupils with special needs to assist them at the toilet, moving between classroom and at break times.

- They identified ways in which children with special needs could join in games and sports. For example, a blind child can be partnered with a sighted child in running competitions.

- Within the class, they developed opportunities for 'peer tutoring'; that is more able pupils assisted the less able learners in class-work (see Chapter 9).

- They devised learning games in which small groups of pupils played together in class. These were designed to master reading and number skills.

- They set the class activities which they had to complete as a group. In this way, all the children can contribute to the completion of the task and gain credit for achieving it.

- They promoted the talents of children with special needs by encouraging their participation in school activities, such as singing, dancing and drama in which they could more easily participate.

- They involved children with special needs in all school activities; for example in cleaning and cooking chores and by having them act as class monitors.

Teachers commented that it was a good sign when they saw children playing happily together at break times and if they were told about pupils visiting each other at home.

IDEAS FOR COMMUNICATING THE MESSAGES

Discuss teachers' usual attitudes to pupils in general. What shapes their attitudes? What are the implications for inclusion? How might teachers' attitudes be changed?

Theme 2: The Layout of Classrooms

It is important for teachers with a class of children of varying abilities to organise the classroom in such a way that all learners can benefit. Some possible factors to consider in the classroom are:

- Children with special needs should sit close to the teacher and the chalkboard. The child can then see and hear the teacher better and the teacher can more easily check their work and control their behaviour.

- Teachers should stand in the brightest part of the room so that all pupils can see them more easily.

- Try to arrange the room so that children can move freely, especially if some have visual problems or use mobility aids.

- Make sure any dangerous materials and equipment are kept in a cupboard or on a high shelf.

- The children's desks can be arranged in groups so that those of the same ability can work together.

- If space permits, try to set aside an area of the classroom so that you can work with certain children on a one-to-one basis or in small groups for short periods. This area could be screened off using a moveable screen to reduce the distractions for the child.

- Have a variety of activities which children can use if they have completed their work ahead of others. This could include a small library of books, worksheets and games.

- Display charts and posters at children's eye-level rather than high up on the walls. Use large writing, pictures and symbols so that these are easily seen and understood by all children. You can also add different textures for touching to help children with visual problems.

- Some learning is better done outside of classrooms. Using money to buy food can be done in a pretend way in the classroom but even better if children with special needs have the opportunity to practice in real settings. Likewise lessons about plants and animals could be done in the school grounds or neighbouring farms.

- Children with visual and hearing problems may find it more difficult to learn if classes are held out-of-doors. Schools may have to arrange for teachers to have suitable rooms if they have such children in their class particularly when they are just starting school.

IDEAS FOR COMMUNICATING THE MESSAGES

Programme 5 in the DVD *Inclusion in Action* (also downloadable through YouTube, see p.11) illustrates how teachers can use small groupings of pupils as a means of coping with different ability levels within a class. Teachers can discuss the advantages and disadvantages of doing this within their classrooms. What would encourage them to try it, if they have not already used this approach?

Theme 3: Lesson Planning

The time teachers spend in preparing a lesson is time well spent. This makes the class easier to manage and the teaching more effective for all learners. Preparation is especially necessary when there are pupils with special needs in the class. Planning may not take much time; 10 minutes can suffice.

- When planning a lesson, teachers need to think of the outcomes they are setting for the class as a whole and then for certain individual pupil. The Individual Plans will help here (see Chapter 9). Teachers are then able to adjust the lesson and the work you want the children with special needs to do according to their abilities. For example, the class may be doing simple addition but one pupil may be given five sums rather than ten to do while another may be working at a simpler level again – counting objects into sets. Hence in the one lesson, the teacher works at different levels according to the child's abilities. This is known as differentiation of the curriculum.

- Some children learn better through doing things particularly slow learners. Think how children can be actively involved in the lesson. For example, in learning about measurement, the children can find out each other's height!

- Also children with special needs will be able to understand better if they can see and feel objects. Are there visual aids you can use in your lessons? These can be real objects, photographs, drawings and posters.

- Decide the key words to be used in the lesson. List these for the class at the beginning of the lesson and check that the pupils understand their meaning.

- Worksheets can be prepared for the special needs children to use during the lesson. These can be designed to meet their particular needs, such as large print if they have visual impairments, or simplified for those with learning disabilities. You can keep them for future use by covering them with sticky-backed plastic to make them more durable. Teachers can swop worksheets with colleagues.

- Group work facilitates participation of all learners and is an excellent way of responding to individual needs. With special needs pupils, you may need to give them a lesson suited to their needs and leave them to do work on this while you teach an expanded or another lesson to the rest of the class.

- Teachers may need to adjust the pace of the lesson and the amount of material they cover in the time available. It is better to be selective than try to cover too much material.

- As well as individual lesson plans, teachers also need to make a plan for the school day. This will note the alternative activities for children with special needs. It can be helpful to share this plan with pupils at the beginning of lessons. Also lessons that may be more difficult for the class should come earlier in the day when they are likely to be more alert.

> IDEAS FOR COMMUNICATING THE MESSAGES
>
> - Programme 5 in the DVD Inclusion in Action has a model lesson of a teacher teaching simple addition. View the lesson and have participants note the various ways the teacher had prepared the lesson in advance. This is also available on YouTube (see p.11).
> - Then ask participants to prepare a lesson plan for a topic of their choosing. Invite them to share their plans with one another and get feedback on them.

Theme 4: Child-to-Child/Peer Tutoring

The pupils in the class are an important learning resource overlooked by many teachers. Teachers can mobilise this resource for the benefit of learners with special needs but all pupils stand to benefit.

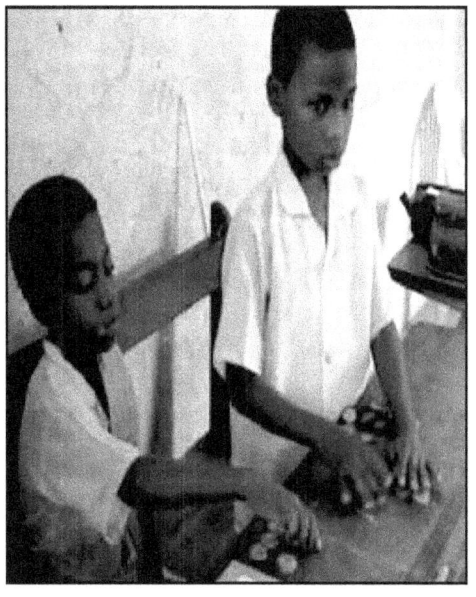

Peer tutoring involves pairing a competent learner with the one having difficulty in one particular subject. For example a student who is good at number work can be paired with a student who is having difficulties. When the competent student has finished the work that was set by the teacher, he or she can help a weaker student to complete the assignment. This will give the more able student an opportunity to consolidate their learning as well as providing the weaker student with individual assistance.

However, wider benefits also flow. Peer tutors provide role models for disruptive pupils. They will give shyer student more confidence and encourage their self-esteem. Learners may be more willing to ask questions with peer tutors than they would with teachers. It fosters a spirit of co-operation within a class.

Peer tutors also benefit. They may become more observant, better communicators and more patient. Their self-confidence is also boosted. Some peer tutors have later trained as teachers.

- Teachers should select the peer tutors carefully. As well as being more capable they should also have a kind nature and not be pupils who will bully or be nasty to the weaker student.

- Peer tutors are there to encourage the learner to do the work. They are not there to do it for them. This needs to be made clear right from the start.

- Teachers need to give the peer tutor examples of how they should work with the weaker student and discreetly monitor them doing this. They need to give plenty of praise when they do well, alongside correcting their mistakes.

- If possible recruit different peer tutors to work with the child, for example in different subjects. This ensures they do not become over-dependent on one tutor. The group of peer tutors might be given some preparation together prior to tutoring.

- It is helpful if teachers have prepared worksheets for the learner as these provide a guide that the peer tutors can follow.

- Peer tutors and partners should also experience taking part in fun activities together – games, dancing, singing – so that it is not all work!

- The pair can also work together on sports activities; competing on the same team.

- Teachers should consider pupils with special needs as peer tutors for other learners in the class. For example students who are wheelchair users and proficient in reading may assist other students with their reading.

- If a peer tutor is finding their role stressful, teachers should discretely reallocate them to another learner or give them other responsibilities.

- Teachers should inform the parents of peer tutors of the contribution they are making to the class and allay any misconceptions they may have. Likewise the Head Teacher and colleagues need to be supportive of using peer tutors.

IDEAS FOR COMMUNICATING THE MESSAGES

- Peer tutoring may be a new concept for most teachers. If possible find a teacher with experience of using it in his/her class and invite them to give a workshop for other teachers.
- Encourage teachers to think how they might try-out some peer tutoring with their class and identify any likely pit-falls they might need to avoid.

Theme 5: Managing Disruptive Behaviours

A major concern of teachers is that learners with special needs will be disruptive in class. This is not always true. Often the more disruptive pupils are not those with special needs. But in either case, the teacher needs to be able to manage inappropriate behaviours if pupils are to learn.

Among the disruptive behaviours which teachers commonly report are: not sitting still, easily distracted, disturbing or interfering with other pupils, not following instructions and being aggressive.

All pupils need to learn to behave in a socially acceptable way. And nearly all can learn to do this if teachers are firm and consistent in the way they manage behaviours. It is an admission of failure on the part of the teacher and the school if a pupil has to be asked to leave because of disruptive behaviours.

Managing a child's behaviour involves three basic approaches. 1. Reinforcing 'good' behaviour; 2. Ignoring inappropriate behaviours and 3. Time-out when the child is removed from the situation so that the behaviour no longer affects others and the child regains self-control.

Here are the strategies that African teachers have found to be effective based around these three approaches:

- All the teachers (and others) involved with the pupil at school agree a common approach to reacting to the child's behaviour, especially in the use of rewards and punishments.

- Can you identify a cause for the child's behaviour? Are they trying to avoid doing work they find difficult? Do they like getting attention from the other children and the teachers? Are they restless because of hunger? Observing and recording when the behaviour occurs may give some clues as to its cause and the action that is most appropriate for you to take.

- The child may benefit from a shorter school day or having times to themselves when they can rest. It is better the pupil behaves appropriately all of the time he or she is in class than be in class behaving inappropriately. The length of time the child stays in class can be gradually increased. This strategy is useful when first introducing children to new classes.

- You might re-position the child in the class. Children who are inclined to run around, could be seated next to the wall or between two other pupils so that cannot move so easily.

- Active children can be given meaningful tasks to do such as giving out worksheets and tidying the room.

- Teachers should reward the child when he or she is behaving appropriately and has successfully completed the work set. Do this through praise, class recognition and perhaps the award of a 'gold' star. When children have five stars they can exchange them for a treat, such as fruit. Any plan for dealing with inappropriate behaviours MUST include the encouragement of positive behaviours. Otherwise the children learn what they are not to do, but they have not learnt what they should do.

- Rewards often work best when the whole class earns a 'treat' for good behaviour. This puts 'peer pressure' on disruptive pupils to behave appropriately.

- Pupils will often show warning signs of disruptive behaviour starting. If you can identify these, try to divert the child: for example move closer and put your hand on his shoulder as you continue with the lesson. Or have the child do an activity you know he is capable of and enjoys doing; for example, giving out books to the class.

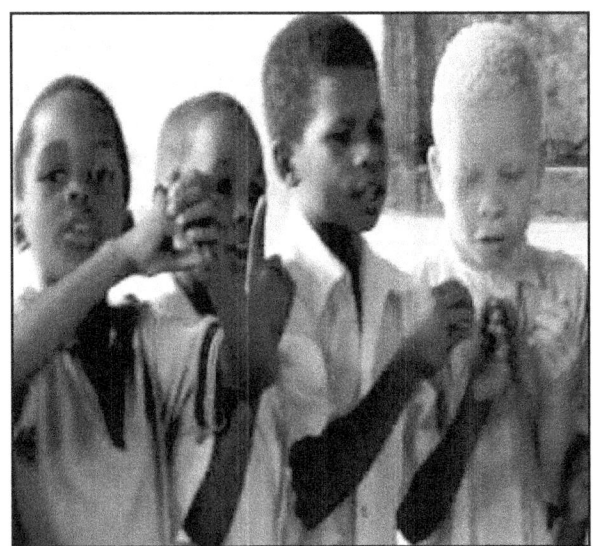

- Use tone of voice, facial expression and short, simple sentences to convey your displeasure at pupil's behaviour. Remain calm and in control.

- Punishments are only effective if children can understand the link between them and their behaviour and if it is something they do not like. Having children stand outside the classroom may be a reward to the child who wants to avoid schoolwork! Likewise do not use extra schoolwork as a punishment. The child will then associate it with bad behaviour!

- Do not threaten the child unless you can carry out the threat and are prepared to do it. Make clear to the child, the consequences of their behaviours. For example, if they hit another pupil, they have to stay in class at lunchtime and not play outside.

- Beware of handing over your authority to others. For example, sending a disruptive pupil to the Head Teacher gives the message that you are not as important as the Head. Both you and the head should see the pupil together.

- Find out from the family if the child shows the same behaviours at home. If so, plan with the carers a common approach to reacting to these behaviours. This consistency at home and school is more likely to help the child to stop behaving inappropriately.

- With more able pupils, encourage discussion of the effects that their behaviours can have on one another. The use of drama and role-play can let pupils experience and release their emotions.

- A method which works with one pupil's behaviour, may not work with another. Planned and consistent responses are the keys to success that take into account the individual pupil's characteristics.

- With particularly severe behaviours the child may need to be withdrawn from the class to work with another adult. However this strategy must form part of a plan in which the suggestions made above feature. Otherwise the pupil may use the behaviour to opt out of class work.

- Schools need to work out a policy on suspending and expelling children from schools because of their behaviour. This means that all teachers are following the same procedures and children are being treated fairly. The policy should describe the unacceptable behaviours; the actions that will be taken by class teachers and the school; the contact with families and the length of time the child can be suspended.

- Some children's behaviour is due to emotional problems or reactions to bad experiences. They may benefit from seeing a specialist who might be able to identify and help resolve the causes for the behaviour. However we appreciate that such expertise may not be available to many teachers. Nonetheless many of the above strategies will assist the child, allied with a trusted relationship between the learner and teacher.

Teachers sometimes try these strategies but they complain that they did not work. Often they have given up too soon as sometimes children's behaviour worsens when new strategies are started. Hence teachers need to beware of giving up too soon.

> **IDEAS FOR COMMUNICATING THE MESSAGES**
> - Teachers should be encouraged to share the strategies they have found successful for managing classes. This will increase teachers' confidence that they are working along the right lines.
> - Debate the use of punishment within schools. For example, should corporal punishment be banned in schools?

Concluding comment

Although this chapter has focused on how teachers can manage their class, these strategies have to be developed in the context of a whole-school approach to learners with special needs. Therefore, head teachers in particular need to encourage dialogue among their staff on how best to adapt their classroom practices to accommodate the special needs of learners. This can happen at regular staff meetings or at in-service training workshops held with the cooperation and involvement of school inspectors, specialist advisers and colleagues from teacher training institutes.

CHAPTER 11:
Future Challenges

Our primary concern in this book has been the introduction of inclusive education into local schools and communities. We have shown how this can be done even in the most impoverished districts of African countries. But the process of creating an inclusive education system has to be ongoing within and beyond individual schools. There are many books and manuals available to guide these processes. We end by giving a flavour of the two pertinent challenges within an African context. In particular:

– Adapting the curriculum.

– Evaluating Inclusive Education.

Adapting the Curriculum

The relevance of the existing school curriculum in preparing children for modern life is hotly debated in many countries. There is no doubt that an emphasis on a wholly academic curriculum excludes many pupils and not just those with special needs. This is particularly so when children have to pass examinations before they can move on to the next grade within schools: a practice that is now discouraged as it de-motivates learners and increases school drop-outs.

Among the developments taking hold in rich as well as poorer countries, is the provision of a more diversified curriculum in schools. In addition to the traditional academic subjects, this may focus on the personal and social development of pupils, the meaning of citizenship and on practical skills valued within that community such as animal husbandry.

Teachers are also given greater freedom in adjusting the curriculum to meet the needs of pupils; for example including more basic skills for those who are at the early stages of acquiring literacy or numerical competence.

Alternatives to examinations to assess pupil's competence are being considered as written exams tend to disadvantage pupils with special needs. Other options, such as the preparation of portfolios of work are being introduced.

Although teachers may experiment with these new approaches, it is the responsibility of educational authorities to redesign the curriculum and examination systems to make them more inclusive. The pressure for these reforms increases as more children with special needs are enrolled in mainstream schools. Excluding these pupils reduces the need for changing existing school systems and hence the status quo is more likely to be retained.

Preparation for Adulthood

Preparing young people for adulthood is a particular challenge when youth have special needs. They may not be able to meet the demands of an academic curriculum and yet they require extra assistance to master some of the skills needed to participate in community life. Hence in Zanzibar, a joint project was developed between the Parent organisation (ZAPDD) and the Ministry of Education to devise a curriculum that was better suited to youth with disabilities who had dropped out of schools.

The main aim of the Youth Programme was to increase their skills and involvement in all sectors of life. A rights perspective was adopted based on key articles from the UN Convention.

Self-advocacy was promoted and the youth were assisted to become active members in ZAPDD branches. A co-ordinator was appointed to lead the project who was an experienced teacher of special needs children. He was seconded to work on the Project.

> In Lesotho young men become herd boys. The skills needed are simple for non-disabled youth but those with learning difficulties needed to be taught them; such as counting the cattle, knowing the appropriate grazing area, the time for the herd to drink and separating them into each owner's kraal. The tasks were taught as part of their work experience. At first, some villagers abused the youth and only paid them with a plate of food. After further training they practiced negotiating their salaries with minimal assistance.

The Project's activities took place both in schools and outside of schools.

- In schools, opportunities were provided for a more practical (functional) curriculum with a focus on basic life skills that youth with developmental disabilities may lack; such a money skills, reading signs, washing clothes, cooking, gardening and looking after animals.

- The learners are encouraged to practice their skills in the local community; for example, enlisting the help of local stall-holders as they learn money skills.

- In school, but more importantly outside of school, the young people are helped to acquire the skills needed in farming and in making crafts. They were taught various vocational skills such as carpentry and rug-making.

- For the youth who have dropped out of school, youth clubs are organised. One club started an income generating project of making roof thatch and sweeping brooms which they sold to local people. One young physically disabled lady was so successful at making door mats and baskets that she earned enough to support her elderly parents.

- The clubs also provided opportunities to talk to the young people about issues such as HIV and AIDS. Drama and role plays were used to get across the message. They were encouraged to make friends with one another so that they could socialise in their neighbourhoods.

> In some countries disabled youth and children are sexually abused by HIV/AIDS victims who are told by some traditional healers that the diseases will be cured if they sleep with a disabled girl. Youth need to know how to protect themselves. They need to be told about sexually transmitted diseases and the use of condoms. Trainers should talk openly about sex, using visual aids and models. They should answer questions honestly and encourage the young people to share their experiences.

- The youth were encouraged to speak up for their rights. They have devised dramas to raise awareness of issues that affect young people with disabilities. They learnt how to cope with bullying: to walk away and not to confront the abuser but to talk to somebody who can assist in the matter. They took part in community gatherings aimed at educating certain groups such as taxi drivers who do not stop for people in wheel-chairs.

- Sports and leisure activities also feature in the clubs. Able-bodied students play alongside their peers with disabilities in football and basketball. As well as being fun, sports and games like tug-of-war provide opportunities for the young people to develop social interaction and team-working skills, following rules, controlling their emotions, increase their physical fitness and co-ordination skills.

- The young people learnt how to use local transport – buses and taxis – to get from home to the Club. They had to learn road safety as well as which bus to board, pay the correct fare, and know when to get off. Teachers accompanied them at first but later, they practiced alone and teachers waited at the destination for them.

- The young people became peer tutors or assistants for one another. This helped them to become more understanding of others and friendships developed. For example, one lady with mild intellectual disability was paired with another learner who had a visual impairment. She would guide her from home to the club which meant crossing a river and some busy roads.

- Being able to earn money is important for all young people when they leave school. Hence in schools and in youth clubs opportunities are sought for young people to experience working in community settings such as cycle repairing and carpentry. Others experienced brick making, welding, painting and working as a handy man in mechanics.

Throughout there were close links between the programme, schools and families. For example youth undertook work experience in family businesses such as running a food stall.

A youth with intellectual disability from a family of three who was the eldest was trained in domestic work and gardening with mastery of both skills. He became the bread winner after both his parents died. He looked after the siblings; and provided food, clothing and education. His siblings both completed their secondary education and went on to train professionally. His sister went for nursing and the brother trained in painting.

The benefits

These are some of the benefits that were observed:

- A growth in self-confidence among the youth. They took better care over their appearance.

- A reduction in inappropriate behaviours.

- The young people were able to do more things around the home – fetching water, looking after animals - and parents expected more of them.

- The young people were more productively occupied rather than lying around at home.

- They were better communicators.

- They became decision-makers as they were consulted on the activities and the programmes provided in the club.

IDEAS FOR COMMUNICATING THE MESSAGES

The DVD *Inclusion in Action* has a sixth programme that describes the Youth Programme. This is also available on YouTube (see p.11). This could be used to trigger discussion about the changes that are needed to the present school curriculum in order to better prepare young people for an adult life in their local community.

Concluding comments

If school do not change, then new forms of 'learning centres' may need to be established outside of educational systems to provide particular forms of education and training that are better suited to pupils' needs, such as artisan schools and vocational training centres.

Learning need not stop at an arbitrary school leaving age but life-long learning opportunities will become more available to everyone through new forms of educational provision. Again these will benefit people who may be slow learners.

Perhaps the traditional teaching workforce will be augmented by enlisting the expertise of experienced practitioners across many disciples and professions as they mentor or supervise young people who are placed with them on work experience.

In sum, the future holds much promise. Teachers need to be to the fore in instigating innovative practices and advocating for improvements to systems that are not suited to modern needs.

Evaluating Inclusive Education

How can we know that inclusive education is effective? This commonly asked question has no ready answer. Some people ask it as a reason for NOT making schools inclusive. They want to have the evidence before they decide but equally they may not be satisfied with the results they are given.

Others ask the question because they want to know the outcomes from implementing inclusive education. But people may not agree as to which outcomes are important. Is it increased enrolments of pupils with special needs, or better results in examinations or changes in the attitudes of teachers or .... indeed the list can go on and on.

Perhaps the most productive approach to the question is to focus not on outcomes but rather on the processes that help to make inclusive education effective and those that act as barriers. It is the latter approach that was used in the three African countries. This is sometimes known as a 'formative evaluation' as the main goal is to uncover how the topic under investigation was formed and shaped through the experience of implementing it (Gosling and Edwards, 1995).

Two main approaches were used. First, the team leading the implementation continually reviewed and evaluated their work. Second, outside reviewers were invited to visit the projects to meet with key personnel and observe practice within schools. Both approaches are commended as they complement one another.

Ongoing monitoring

The team involved with implementing inclusive education was able to evaluate their achievements based on the following information.

- They kept records of the various consultation meetings that had been held and the decisions taken.
- They filed all the relevant papers and reports they had prepared.
- The schools kept records of the pupils with special needs that had been enrolled and also a record of attendances.
- The school kept notes of the meetings of the Inclusive Education Committee.
- The team collected all the materials used in the training events they held for teachers. They recorded the attendance by teachers and had them complete evaluation sheets to get their feedback.
- The team regularly visited school to consult with head teachers and observe teachers undertaking lessons. They provided feedback to the teachers and head teachers.
- The team held regular meetings to review progress and adjust their planning in light of emerging needs.
- Annual progress reports were prepared for the Ministry of Education and the funders of the programme.

External review

In all three countries, external personnel were invited by the Ministries and the funders to undertake an external review of the Inclusive Education programme after it had been going for three years. This came towards the end of the pilot phase of the project and prior to the programme being rolled out to further schools. Thus the main lessons from the pilot study could be collated and used to inform the future planning of the programme.

The chosen reviewers were experienced in inclusive education from outside the country and with expertise in working in low-income countries. They could act as a critical friend to the programme staff as well as providing an independent evaluation of the programme's strengths and weaknesses. Their recommendations also helped to guide the further development of the programme and to ensure that the necessary resources were made available.

In preparing for the evaluation, the following steps were needed.

- The terms of reference for the evaluation had to be written. These guided the evaluators as to the main issues on which their opinions were sought. For example, in Lesotho the evaluators were asked to give feedback on the appropriateness of teacher training materials, the overall teaching strategies used and the impact on learners.
- All relevant files and records were made available to the evaluators. This included the national educational policies and agreements that had been made between the Ministry and the funders.
- Arrangements were made for the evaluators to interview key informants in the Ministry and local offices, members of the national steering committee as well as members of

Inclusive Education Committee such as community leaders, health workers, representatives from DPOs and INGOs.

During their visits to the programmes, the evaluators used a participatory approach as far as possible. The attended staff meetings in school, they met with groups of parents and they talked with students with and without disabilities. They observed teachers in the classroom; scrutinised their Individual Education Plans and lesson plans, and the teaching aids they had made.

The evaluators prepared a draft report that summarised the information gathered, the conclusions they had drawn and their recommendations for future action. As a courtesy, the draft was made available to the Inclusive Education Team to comment on its accuracy prior to its formal submission to the Ministry and the funders.

The National Steering Group was tasked with drawing up an implementation plan based on the evaluation report. Among the areas that the evaluators felt required further attention were: greater engagement of schools with parents; improvements in the accessibility within schools; further opportunities for teacher training; recording the educational attainments of pupils with special needs; the dissemination of learning across schools and post-school provision for school-leavers with special needs. Conversely, they commended the multi-sectorial approach used, the efforts made to educate communities, the diversity of children now included in schools, and the emphasis on the whole school.

> #### IDEAS FOR COMMUNICATING THE MESSAGES
> Invite participants to plan an evaluation of Inclusive Education within one school. Who would they talk to? What questions would they ask? Who could they invite as critical friends to provide an outside perspective?

Final thought

We stress again that the main purpose of the evaluation is improve schools and the education they provide to all pupils. It is not to find fault or to apportion blame. No school is perfect and probably never will be. But every school can do better. It is that spirit which needs to infuse educational systems around the world if 'Education for All' is to be achieved.

Further Actions

Although we have come to the end, it is in many ways only the end of the beginning. In this book we have taken you through the critical steps of the conception, birth and nurturing of Inclusive Education. The infant by now is walking and a going concern. Looking ahead it is possible to anticipate further assistance in order to bring Inclusive Education to maturity. In particular:

- Extra resources to improve school buildings and make them fully accessible.

- Improved leadership from head teachers and Boards of Management.

- Ongoing support for teachers within schools to assist with the particular challenges that certain pupils can present.

- Modules on inclusive education need to be included in initial teacher training courses.

- Further in-service training opportunities for teachers so that they can access the wealth of knowledge that is available now on improving schools.

- Reform of examination systems so that all pupils can gain recognition for their achievements.

- Continued learning opportunities after pupils leave school, especially for those with special needs.

- Closer networking of schools with other sectors such as community development, health and social services.

The list may seem never-ending but we repeat the simple motto for making the seemingly impossible possible. Start with what you can change: one child, one class, one school at a time. You may not transform the world but you will have transformed that school.

References and Further Reading

References

Ainscow, M. (1991) Effective Schools for All: An alternative approach to special needs in education. *Cambridge Journal of Education*, 21, 293-308.

Emerson, E., McConkey, R., Walsh, P.N. & Felce, D. (2008) Editorial: Intellectual disability in a global context. *Journal of Policy and Practice in Intellectual Disability*, 5 (2),79-80.

Gosling. L. & Edwards, M. (1995) *Toolkits, practical guide to assessment monitoring review and evaluation*. London: Save the Children UK.

Holloway, S., Lee, L. & McConkey, R. (1999) Meeting the training needs of community-based service personnel in Africa through video-based training courses. *Disability and Rehabilitation*, 21 (9) 448-454.

Hornby, G. (1995) *Working with parents of children with special needs*. London: Cassell.

Khatleli, P., Mariga, L., Phachaka, L. & Stubbs, S. (1995) 'Schools for all: national planning in Lesotho.' In B. O'Toole & R. McConkey (eds), *Innovations in Developing Countries for People with Disabilities*, pp. 135–60. Chorley, UK: Lisieux Hall Publications. Available for free download at: http://www.eenet.org.uk/resources/docs/inno_dev_coun.php

Lewis. I. (2008) *Young Voices: young people's views of inclusive Education*. Published by Atlas Alliance. Available at: http://www.atlas-alliansen.no/English/-Young-voices-DVD-and-photo-brochure.

McConkey, R. & Bradley, A. (2010) Promoting Inclusive Education in Low Income Countries. In V. Timmons and P.N. Walsh. *A Long Walk to School: International Research on Inclusive Education across the Life-Span*. Amsterdam: Sense Publishers.

McConkey, R. & Mariga, L. (2010) Building social capital for inclusive education: Insights from Zanzibar. *Journal of Research in Special Educational Needs*, 11 (1), 12-19.

McConkey, R., Mariga, L., Braadland, N. & Mphole, P. (2000) Parents as trainers about disability in low income countries. *International Journal of Disability, Development and Education*, 47, 309-317.

McConkey, R. & Mphole, P. (2000) Training needs in developing countries: Experiences from Lesotho. *International Journal of Rehabilitation Research*, 23, 119-123.

McConkey, R., O'Toole, B. & Mariga, L. (1999) Educating teachers in developing countries about disabilities, *Exceptionality Education Canada*, 9, 15-38.

Mariga L. & McConkey R. (1987) Home-based learning programmes for mentally handicapped people in rural areas of Zimbabwe. *International Journal of Rehabilitation Research*, 10: 175-183.

Mittler, P (1995) Rethinking partnership between professionals and parents, *Children and Society* 9 (3) 22-40.

Mittler, P. (2012) The UN Convention: Use it or Lose it? *Disability, CBR and Inclusive Development*, 23, 2, 7-21 Free download at: http://dcidj.org/article/view/141/81

O'Toole B. (1988) A community-based rehabilitation programme for preschool disabled children in Guyana. *International Journal of Rehabilitation Research*, 11,32-334.

Peters, S.J. (2004) *Inclusive Education: An EFA Strategy For All Children*. Washington DC: World Bank.

Putnam, R. (2000) *Bowling Alone: The Collapse and Revival of American Community*. New York: Simon and Schuster.

Secretariat for the African Decade of Disabled Persons (2012) Draft Southern Africa Regional Inclusive Education Strategy. Available at: http://african-decade.co.za/miscellaneous/

Stubbs, S. (2008) *Inclusive Education: Where there are few resources*. Oslo: Atlas-Alliance. Available at: http://www.atlas-alliansen.no/English/Inclusive-Education-Where-there-are-few-resources-(updated-edition-2008)

United Nations Educational, Scientific and Cultural Organisation (2002) *Innovations in Non-Formal Education: A Review of Selected Initiatives from the Asia-Pacific Region*. Available at: http://www2.unescobkk.org/elib/publications/INFE/

UNICEF (2006) *Africa's Orphaned and Vulnerable Generations: Children affected by AIDS*. Available at: http://www.unicef.org/publications/index_35645.html

UNICEF (2006) *Management of sick children by community health workers*. Available at: http://www.unicef.org/publications/files/Management_of_Sick_Children_by_Community_Health_Workers.pdf

UNICEF (2010) *Facts for Life. A guide to the top ten health messages for families*. Available at: http://www.unicef.org/publications/index_53254.html

Werner, D. (Undated) *Disabled Village Children*. Available at: http://disabledvillagechildren.projects.unamesa.org/

World Bank (1998) *The Initiative on Defining, Monitoring and Measuring Social Capital: Overview and Program Description. Social Capital Initiative Working Paper, No.1*. Washington: The World Bank.

World Health Organisation (2001). *International Classification of Functioning, Disability and Health*. Geneva: WHO.

WHO, UNESCO, ILO & IDDC (2010). *Community Based Rehabilitation: CBR Guidelines. Introductory Booklet.* Geneva: WHO. Available at: http://www.who.int/disabilities/cbr/guidelines/en/index.html

World Health Organisation & World Bank (2011). *World Report on Disability.* Geneva: WHO. Available at: http://www.who.int/disabilities/world_report/2011/en/index.html

Further Reading on Inclusive Education

Alur, M. & Timmons, V. (2009) *Inclusive Education Across Cultures: Crossing Boundaries, Sharing Ideas,* New Delhi: Sage Publications.

Armstrong, A.C., Armstrong, D. & Spandagou, I. (2010) *Inclusive Education: International Policy & Practice.* London: Sage Publications.

Barron, T. & Amerena, P. (2007) *Disability and Inclusive Development.* London: Leonard Cheshire International.

Clough, P. & Corbett, J. (2000) *Theories of Inclusive Education: A Student's Guide.* London: Paul Chapman Publishing.

Inclusion International (2009) *Better Education for All when we're included too: A Global Report.* London: Inclusion International. Available at: http://ii.gmalik.com/pdfs/Better_Education_for_All_Global_Report_October_2009.pdf

Lansdown, G. (2009) *See Me Hear Me: A Guide to Using Article 24 of the CRPD.* London: Save the Children UK.

Mitchell, D. (2008) *What Really Works in Special and Inclusive Education: Using Evidence-Based Teaching Strategies.* Abingdon, UK: Routledge.

Mitchell, D. (2008) *Contextualizing Inclusive Education: Evaluating old and new international perspectives.* Abingdon, UK: Routledge.

Mittler, P. (2000) *Working towards inclusive education: Social contexts.* London: David Fulton Publishing.

Mittler P (2012). *Overcoming Exclusion: Social Justice through Education.* World Library of Educationalists. London: Routledge.

Rieser, R. (2012) *Implementing Inclusive Education: A Commonwealth Guide to Implementing Article 24 of the UN Convention on the Rights of Persons with Disabilities.* London: Commonwealth Secretariat.

Rose, R. (2010) *Confronting the Obstacles to Inclusion: International Responses to Developing Inclusive Education.* London: David Fulton Publishers and Nasen.

Timmons, V. & Walsh, P.N. (2010). *A Long Walk to School: International Research on Inclusive Education across the Life-Span.* Amsterdam: Sense Publishers.

United Nations Educational, Scientific and Cultural Organisation (2003). *Open File on Inclusive Education: Support Materials for Managers and Administrators.* Paris: UNESCO.

Websites

These two websites have a wealth of resources available on inclusive education:

UNESCO: http://www.unesco.org/new/en/education/themes/strengthening-education-systems/inclusive-education/

Enabling Education Network (EENET): http://www.eenet.org.uk/index.php

International DPOs

Inclusion International (mainly for persons with intellectual and developmental disabilities). http://www.inclusion-international.org/

Disabled Peoples International (DPI). Founded in 1981, it covers five regions: Africa, Asia Pacific, Europe, Latin America, North America and Caribbean, and works in 70 countries. http://www.dpi.org/

Sight savers is an international charity that works with partners to eliminate avoidable blindness and promote equality of opportunity for disabled people in the developing world. http://www.sightsavers.org/

The World Federation of the Deaf represents some 70 million deaf people worldwide. https://wfdeaf.org/

www.ingramcontent.com/pod-product-compliance
Lightning Source LLC
Chambersburg PA
CBHW080848010526
44114CB00018B/2397